HD6508
I4
1965

M9-32

W9-AOG-283

NEW ENGLAND INSTITUTE
OF TECHNOLOGY
LEARNING RESOURCES CENTER

NEW ENGLAND INST
OF TECHNOLOG
LIBRARY

Labor in American Society

SCOTT FORESMAN PROBLEMS IN AMERICAN HISTORY

General Editors: **Edwin Fenton,** *Carnegie Institute of Technology*
David H. Fowler, *Carnegie Institute of Technology*

Volumes in this series:

NEW ENGLAND INSTITUTE
OF TECHNOLOGY
LEARNING RESOURCES CENTER

Labor in American Society

Raymond S. Iman, *Chairman, History Department,*
Benjamin Franklin High School, Rochester, N.Y.

Thomas W. Koch, *Instructor, History Department,*
Benjamin Franklin High School, Rochester, N.Y.

SCOTT, FORESMAN AND COMPANY

COVER DESIGN BY ED BEDNO

Copyright © 1965 by Scott, Foresman and Company,
Glenview, Illinois 60025. All Rights Reserved. Printed
in the United States of America. Regional offices of
Scott, Foresman and Company are located in Atlanta,
Dallas, Glenview, Palo Alto, and Oakland, N.J.

Library of Congress catalog card #65-12431

Editors' Introduction

Growing numbers of history teachers realize that using source materials in their courses provides an added dimension of experience for their students. Total reliance on a textbook can no longer be considered an adequate means of learning history. Yet if the full value of documents and critical articles is to be obtained, they must be presented as something more than writings which record important events or as mere illustrations of what the text says. They must also challenge the student's ability to relate individual events to larger topics and to continuing themes in history.

Each volume of the SCOTT FORESMAN PROBLEMS IN AMERICAN HISTORY organizes source materials around one facet of our nation's past. A volume contains fifteen Problems, each designed for one day's work. In some of the books the Problems are intended to be read individually, at the proper chronological intervals. In others, they are grouped into three units of five Problems each, such a unit being best used as an uninterrupted week's work. Whether the Problems are studied individually or in units, they should be assigned only after the student had read the relevant material in his textbook.

One of the most vital services a collection of source materials can perform is to encourage the student to develop his critical abilities to the utmost in constructing historical explanations. Interpretation is the heart of history; the student should be brought to realize how essential it is to be able to do more with facts than memorize them. The SCOTT FORESMAN PROBLEMS are specifically designed to engage the student in the fascinating task of interpreting American history. Through them he will gain the skills and the enjoyment which come from reaching insight and understanding as well as knowledge of history.

Each Problem begins with an introduction written by the author to place documents in their historical context and to link together the Problems in a volume. These introductions prepare the student to read intelligently by defining the scope of the Problem, suggesting its relationship to larger issues, and pointing out difficulties of interpretation so that he will not attempt the impossible in generalizing from limited evidence.

The study questions at the end of the introduction carry the student further in applying the historian's critical tools. He may be asked to try to judge the reliability of a document or the bias of a critic, to assess an historical interpretation in the light of his knowledge, or to reason from particulars to a general conclusion of his own. Properly used, the study questions help beginning students find out what is important in source materials; without them, students often do not know what they are supposed to do with the readings.

To obtain more from a Problem than simply answers to the author's questions, the student should first read the introduction and questions and then pause to review what he already knows about the subject. Then, keeping the central issues in mind, he should study the entire Problem, perhaps first skimming through it to see the relationship of the parts to the whole, and then reading it carefully and taking notes. He will then be ready to consider his answers to the study questions in preparation for class discussion.

The teacher can use the SCOTT FORESMAN PROBLEMS in several ways. A Problem can perhaps serve most effectively as the basis for discussion by an entire class, with the lesson organized around the study questions or other questions proposed by the teacher to develop new points of view. What seems most appropriate for discussion will always depend partly upon the textbook used in the course and partly upon the instructor's own style of teaching and command of the subject. Each teacher should structure the discussion around those issues which he thinks are most important, but he should take care to link a Problem to those which precede and which follow it. These connecting links give the student the maximum opportunity to comprehend the theme of the volume. By treating a limited number of issues within each Problem, a teacher should be able to restrict discussion to one class period.

These volumes can be used in other ways. Many readings can serve as the basis for reports to the class by individual students. An entire volume, or a selection of Problems from a volume, may be used in preparing a controlled research paper; the three-unit volumes are especially suited to this purpose. The Problems may also be assigned as supplementary reading in those areas where text treatment is not extensive.

In *Labor in American Society,* Raymond S. Iman and Thomas W. Koch examine the history of American working people. In presenting the story of organized labor, the authors have included fascinating material about the lives and opinions of workers drawn from diverse sources. On the whole, readings have been chosen that voice the aspirations and fears of the workers in their own words. Students who use this volume are certain to gain a new appreciation of the struggles of American workers and of their contributions to our society.

EDWIN FENTON
DAVID H. FOWLER

PUBLISHER'S NOTE: The readings in this volume show capitalization and spellings of words, as well as sentence punctuation, as they appear in the sources from which they were taken. Thus, although the Problem introductions and headnotes are according to Scott, Foresman and Company editorial style, many of the readings are not. Omissions from the original texts are shown by ellipses, and interpolations, supplied by the author or editors for clarity, appear in brackets.

Table of Contents

Authors' Introduction

Three periods of labor history are emphasized in many American history textbooks: the Jacksonian era, in which demands of workers became increasingly vocal; the late nineteenth-century rivalry between the Knights of Labor and the American Federation of Labor; and the rise of the Congress of Industrial Organizations in more recent times. Names such as Powderly, Gompers, and Lewis are prominent in traditional accounts of the rise of unions, but many significant people, as well as crucial events, receive only passing attention.

This volume of the SCOTT FORESMAN PROBLEMS IN AMERICAN HISTORY series strives to present a rounded and realistic picture of labor in American society. In most American families a worker has been the major breadwinner. The lives and aspirations of these workers are as important as those of labor leaders, owners of factories, government officials, and other familiar figures. By the use of first-hand accounts, which serve as "contemporary eyes," the stories of these everyday Americans are dramatically presented.

One main theme unites the Problems in the book: the struggle of American workers to improve conditions under which they worked and to better their society more generally. American workers have not only been members of unions—they have also been members of the community at large, involved in a host of problems not associated directly with their working lives. These problems deserve as much attention as the bitter story of strikes and violence, which too often fills the pages of labor history.

The history of labor reveals a great deal about wider American society. The treatment of early workers, such as indentured servants and redemptioners, throws light upon the primitive conditions against which our early settlers were forced to struggle. The aspirations of workers during the Jacksonian period illustrate as much about the problems of a young democracy as they do about labor itself. The struggle between the Knights of Labor and the A.F. of L. reflects the varied responses of free men to the problems of an emerging industrial society. The entire history of government regulation of labor demonstrates the ways in which one interest group affects the society of which it is a part. While we study the role of labor in American society, we also are involved in a study of America itself.

One small volume cannot cover all the major topics in a field as broad as the history of labor in America, nor does this book pretend to furnish a complete history of the labor movement. We have chosen to concentrate on a limited number of subjects rather than to cover superficially many more. Hence, we have not investigated the contribution of Negro slaves to the American labor force nor have we examined the role of the Supreme Court in labor disputes. Both these topics are covered in other volumes of the SCOTT FORESMAN PROBLEMS series. Our hope is that the opportunity to investigate fewer topics in depth will compensate for necessary omissions. By including several interpretations and alternative points of view, we have also attempted to give as fair a representation as possible of controversial subjects. The history of labor in America has often been filled with strife and bitterness. Yet it also stands as a classic example of the way in which participants in a competitive market economy have solved their problems democratically. This volume examines some of the strife and some of the bitterness. It also traces the history of free men operating within the free institutions which have been the pride of Americans. The strife along the way has undoubtedly been part of the price they pay for freedom.

RAYMOND S. IMAN
THOMAS W. KOCH

PROBLEM 1

Workers in Early America

During the seventeenth and eighteenth centuries colonists who came to America faced the problem of recruiting an adequate labor force. Although the entire family served as the basic labor unit, other hands were needed for the many tasks confronting newcomers to these primitive surroundings. The Spanish in Central and South America pressed Indians into service. Since Indians south of the Rio Grande lived in towns or cities and practiced agriculture and handicraft, they were able to make the transition to life among the colonists. In most of North America, however, the Indians were still hunters who roamed across the continent in search of game. Unsuited to the city or farm, they ran away or died when forced into labor. Consequently, workers were recruited from another source. In some areas Negroes, who originally worked under systems of indenture but later became slaves, constituted a part of the colonial labor force.

During the entire colonial period more than half of all persons who came to the Colonies were servants. They were of two types. The majority were indentured servants who sold their services for a number of years, usually seven, in return for passage to America. The Virginia Company first used this type of contract or agreement in the seventeenth century. Beginning early in the eighteenth century, redemptioners joined the ranks. A redemptioner was a man who had insufficient resources to pay for passage and contracted with a shipowner to transport him, and very often his whole family, across the Atlantic. Upon arrival they either found a person who could complete payment for their transportation, or else they permitted the ship's captain to sell their services for a number of years. Most redemptioners came from the Continent, although many arrived from England and Ireland later in the century.

Thousands of Americans came to the New World as servants. They represented all walks of life. Many redemptioners had been well-established farmers or craftsmen; some of the indentured servants were debtors, criminals, or runaway youths.

Not always did they enter into their indentures voluntarily or willingly, nor were they universally accepted in all of the Colonies. Strait-laced New England farmers, for example, who did not need the services of these newcomers as did settlers in other areas, were less inclined to accept their labor. In the middle and southern Colonies, however, they were welcomed and they contributed significantly to the economies of these sections.

Most of these people settled in the Colonies. They worked for their freedom, established families, and eventually blended into the general society. In the seventeenth and eighteenth centuries this type of servitude involved no permanent loss of social position. In both England and America the institution was regarded as a normal way of getting out of debt or of obtaining passage to the American continent. Many of the most prominent families in America trace their descent from men and women who were brought to this country, pledged to work for a number of years in a system of bound labor.

The selections which follow are designed to offer a picture of indentured servants and redemptioners taken mainly from contemporary accounts. As you read, think about the following questions:

1   What did a master gain from an indenture? What did a servant gain? a ship's captain?

2   How were indentured servants treated? How accurately can you generalize from these documents?

3   Do you think that indentured servitude was the best available system of labor for the economy of a new country? Why? Would more widespread Negro slavery have better suited the needs of the early American colonists?

4   To what extent do you agree with Smith's analysis of indentured servitude contained in the last reading?

I

LIFE ABOARD SHIP

The first selection, written by an English observer of American life, describes the arrival of redemptioners in Philadelphia. Although the account was written in the nineteenth century, the events described were typical of earlier years as well. Note the variety of crafts and skills represented in the group. ❏ *Henry Bradshaw Fearon, A Narrative of a Journey of Five Thousand Miles Through America, pp. 148-150. London: Longman, Hurst, Rees, Orme, and Brown, 1818.*

A practice which has been often referred to in connection with this country, naturally excited my attention. It is that of individuals emigrating from Europe without money, and paying for their passage by binding themselves to the captain, who receives the produce of their labour for a certain number of years.

Seeing the following advertisement in the newspapers, put in by the captain and owners of the vessel referred to, I visited the ship, in company with a boot-maker of this city:

"On board the brig Bubona, from Amsterdam, and who are willing to engage themselves for a limited time, to defray the expences of their passage, consist of persons of the following occupations, besides women and children, viz. 13 farmers, 2 bakers, 2 butchers, 8 weavers, 3 taylors, 1 gardener, 3 masons, 1 mill-sawyer, 1 white-smith, 2 shoe-makers, 3 cabinet-makers, 1 coal-burner, 1 barber, 1 carpenter, 1 stocking-weaver, 1 cooper, 1 wheelwright, 1 brewer, 1 locksmith.—Apply on board of the Bubona, opposite Callowhill-street, in the river Delaware, or to W. ODLIN and Co. No. 38, South Wharves."

Oct. 2.

As we ascended the side of this hulk, a most revolting scene of want and misery presented itself. The eye involuntarily turned for some relief from the horrible picture of human suffering, which this living sepulchre afforded. Mr. —— enquired if there were any shoe-makers on board. The captain advanced: his appearance bespoke his office; he is an American, tall, determined, and with an eye that flashes with Algerine cruelty. He called in the Dutch language for shoe-makers, and never can I forget the scene which followed. The poor fellows came running up with unspeakable delight, no doubt anticipating a relief from their loathsome dungeon. Their clothes, if rags deserve that denomination, actually perfumed the air. Some were without shirts, others had this article of dress, but of a quality as coarse as the worst packing cloth. I enquired of several if they could speak English. They smiled and gabbled, 'No Engly, no Engly,—one Engly talk ship.' The deck was filthy. The cooking, washing, and necessary departments were close together. Such is the mercenary barbarity of the Americans who are engaged in this trade that they crammed into one of those vessels 500 passengers, 80 of whom died on the passage. The price for women is about 70 dollars, men 80 dollars, boys 60 dollars. When they saw at our departure that we had not purchased, their countenances fell to that standard of stupid gloom which seemed to place them a link below rational beings.

II

THE SALE OF LABOR

The next reading is from the memoirs of Gottlieb Mittelberger, who came to Pennsylvania in 1750 as a schoolmaster and organist. He describes the shipboard transactions for German redemptioners and the tragic separations which often occurred as a result of the traffic in human labor. □ Gottlieb Mittelberger, *Journey to Pennsylvania in the Year 1750 and Return to Germany in the Year 1754,* trans. Carl Theo. Eben, pp. 26–27, 28–29. Philadelphia: John Jos. McVey, 1898.

The sale of human beings in the market on board the ship is carried on thus: Every day . . . people come from the city of Philadelphia and other places . . . and go on board the newly arrived ship that has brought and offers for sale passengers from Europe, and select among the healthy persons such as they deem suitable for their business, and bargain with them how long they will serve for their passage money, which most of them are still in debt for. When they have come to an agreement, it happens that adult persons bind themselves in writing to serve 3, 4, 5, or 6 years for the amount due by them, according to their age and strength. But very young people, from 10 to 15 years, must serve till they are 21 years old.

Many parents must sell and trade away their children like so many head of cattle; for if their children take the debt upon themselves, the parents can leave the ship free and unrestrained; but as the parents often do not know where and to what people their children are going, it often happens that such parents and children, after leaving the ship, do not see each other again for many years, perhaps no more in all their lives. . . .

It often happens that whole families, husband, wife, and children, are separated by being sold to different purchasers, especially when they have not paid any part of their passage money.

When a husband or wife has died at sea, when the ship has made more than half of her trip, the survivor must pay or serve not only for himself or herself but also for the deceased.

When both parents have died over half-way at sea, their children, especially when they are young and have nothing to pawn or to pay, must stand for their own and their parents' passage, and serve till they are 21 years old. When one has served his or her term, he or she is entitled to a new suit of clothes at parting; and if it has been stipulated, a man gets in addition a horse, a woman, a cow. . . .

If some one in this country runs away from his master, who has treated him harshly, he cannot get far. . . . He who detains or returns a deserter receives a good reward.

If such a runaway has been away from his master one day, he must serve for it as a punishment a week, for a week a month, and for a month half a year. But if the master will not keep the runaway after he has got him back, he may sell him for so many years as he would have to serve him yet.

III

AN INDENTURED SERVANT ON A SOUTHERN PLANTATION

John Harrower emigrated to the Colonies from Scotland in 1773. His indenture was purchased by a Virginia planter who engaged him as a teacher. This excerpt from a letter written to his wife in 1774, presented here in its original form, retains the flavor of the Scottish dialect peculiar to Harrower's birthplace. □ "Diary of John Harrower," *American Historical Review*, Vol. 6, No. 1, October, 1900, pp. 83–84.

BELVIDERA 14.th June 1774.

My Dearest Life
 . . . I shall now aquant you w^t my situation in this Country. I am now settled with . . . [one] Colonel W^m. Dangerfield Esqr. of Belvidera, on the Banks of the River Rappahannock about 160 miles from the Capes or sea mouth, and seven Miles below the Toun of Fredericksburgh. My business is to teach his Children to read write and figure, Edwin his oldest son about 8 years of [age] Bathurest his second 6 years of age and William his youngest son 4 years of age. he has also a Daughter whose name is Hanna Basset. I came to this place on Thursday 26th May and next morning I received his

three sons into my charge to teach, the two youngest boys I got in A : B : C. and the oldest Just begun to syllab and I have now the two youngest spelling and the oldest reading. I am obliged to teach in the English method which was a little aquard to me at first but now quite easy. I am also obliged to talk English the best I can, for Lady Dangerfield speacks nothing but high english, and the Colonel hade his Education in England and is a verry smart Man. As to my agreement it is as follows Viz^t. I am obliged to continue with Col^l. Dangerfield for four years if he insists on it, and for teaching his own children I have Bed, Board, washing and all kind of Cloaths during the above time, and for what schoolars I can get more than his Children I have five shillings currency Quarter for each of them, which is equall to four shillings sterling, and I expect ten or twelve to school next week, for after I hade been here eight days and my abilities and my behavior sufficiently tried, the Colonel rode through the neighbouring Gentlemen and Planters in order to procure scollars for me, so that I hope in a short time to make something of it. And as I have no Occasion to spend a farthing on myself every shill^g. I make shall be carefully remitted you, for your support and my Dear Infants. But I must be some time here before any thing can be done, for you know every thing must have a beginning.

As to my living I eat at their own table, and our witualls are all Dressed in the English taste. we have for Breackfast either Coffie or Jaculate, and warm Loaf bread of the best floor, we have also at table warm loaf bread of Indian corn, which is extreamly good but we use the floor bread always at breackfast. for Dinner smoack'd bacon or what we cal pork ham is a standing dish either warm or cold. when warm we have greens with it, and when cold we have sparrow grass. we have also either warm roast pigg, Lamb, Ducks, or chickens, green pease or any thing else they fancy. As for Tea there is none drunk by any in this Government since I^st. June last, nor will they buy a 2^ds worth of any kind of east India goods, which is owing to the difference at present betwixt the Parliment of great Britton and the North Americans about laying a tax on the tea; and I'm afraid if the Parliment do not give it over it will cause a total revolt as all the North Americans are determined to stand by one another, and resolute on it that they will not submit. I have the news paper sent me to school regularly every week by the Col^l.—Our family consists of the Col^l. his Lady and four Children a housekeeper an Overseer and myself all white. But how many blacks young and old the Lord only knows for I believe there is about thirty that works every day in the field besides the servants about the house; such as Gardner, livery men and pages, Cooks, washer and dresser, sewster and waiting girle. They wash here the whitest that ever I seed for they first Boyle all the Cloaths with soap, and then wash them, and I may put on clean linen every day if I please. My school is a neate little House 20 foot long and 12 foot wide and it stands by itself at the end of an Avenue of planting about as far from the main house as Rob. Forbes is from the burn, and there comes a bonny black bairn every morning to clean it out and make my bed, for I sleep in it by myself. I have a verry fine feather bed under me, and a pair of sheets, a thin fold of a Blanket and a Cotton bed spread is all my bed cloaths, and I find them just enough. as for myself I suppose you wou'd scarce know me now, there being nothing either brown, blew, or black about me but the head and feet, I being Dressed in short cloath Coat, vest Coat, and britches all made of white cotton without any lyning and thread stockins and wearing my own hair curled round like a wigg. at present a suite of Cloaths costs five and twenty shillings here of making which I really think verry high.

IV

TWO INDENTURE CONTRACTS

The terms and obligations of the indenture contract varied with the region and the nature of the work to be done. The basic provisions of these agreements, however, were very similar throughout the American colonies. Following is an indenture of 1713 covering an apprentice in Massachusetts. ☐ *Historical Collections of the Essex Institute*, I, pp. 14–15. Salem, Mass.: Henry Whipple and Son, 1859.

This Indenture, Made the first Day of September, RRae, Annae Nunc Magnae Brittaniae Duodecimo annoq Dom., 1713, Wittnesseth that Nicholas Bourguess, a youth of Guarnsey, of his own free and voluntary will, and by and with the Consent of his present Master, Capt, John Hardy, of Guarnsey, aforesaid, Marriner, hath put himselfe a Servant vnto Mr. William English, of Salem, in the County of Essex, within the Province of the Massachusetts Bay in New England, Marriner, for the space of four yeares from the Day of the Date hereof, vntill the aforesaid Terme of four yeares be fully Compleat & Ended, During all which time the said Servant his said Master his heires, Executors, administrators or assignees Dwelling within the province aforesaid, shall well and faithfully serve, their lawful commands obey; he shall not absent himselfe from his or their service without Leave or Lycense first had from him or them; his Master's Money, goods or other Estate he shall not Purloine, embezzle or wast; at unlawfull Games he shall not Play; Tavernes or Alehouses he shall not Frequent; . . . [evil] he shall not Committ, nor

Matrimony Contract; but in all things shall Demean himselfe as a faithfull Servant During the Terme aforesaid, and the aforesaid Master, on his part, doth for himselfe, his heires and assignees, Covenant, promise and agree to and with the said Servant; that he or they shall and will provide & find him with sufficient Meat, Drink, Cloathing, washing & Lodging, & in Case of Sickness, with Phisick, and attendance During the Terme aforesaid, and to Learn him to read a Chapter well in the bible, if he may be capable of Learning it, & to Dismiss him with two suits of Apparell for all parts of his Body—the one for Lord's Days, the other for working Days.

In Testimony & for Confirmation whereof the parties aforenamed have Interchangeably set their hands and Seales the Day & Yeare first above written.

NICOLLAS BOURGAIZE,

SIGNED, SEALED & DELIVERED IN PRESENCE OF US,—   JOHN HARDY.
MARG'T SEWALL, JUN'R, SUSANNAH SEWALL,
STEPHEN SEWALL, NOT. PUB. & JUSTICE PEACE.

The following selection is an indenture, or agreement, between a Virginia planter and a woman servant. □ From the Maryland State Hall of Records, Annapolis, Maryland.

This Indenture made the 24th day of August in the Yeare of our Lord 1659 betweene Richard Smyth of Virginia Planter of the one parte And Margarett Williams of Bristoll Spinster of the other parte, Wittnesseth that the said Margarett doth hereby Covenant promise and grant to and with the said Richard his Executors & Assignes from the day of the date hereof, vntill her first and next arrivall at Virginea, and after for and during the tearme of ffower yeares to serue in such service, and imploy-ment as the said Richard or his Assignes shall there imploy her, according to the Custome of the Countrey in the like kind. In consideration whereof the said Master doth hereby covenant and grant to and with the said Servant to pay for her passing, and to find and allow her meate, drinke, apparrell and lodging with other Necessaries during the said tearme, And at the end of the said tearme to pay vnto her One Ax one Howe, double Apparrell fifty acres of land one yeares provision according to the custome of the Countrey In wittnes whereof the parties abouenamed to these Indentures haue inter-changeably sett their hands and Seales the day and yeare aboue written

SEALED & DD IN PᴱSENCE OF GEO. HAWKINS   MD WORTH
THE MARKE OF MARGARETT WILLIAMS

V

A MODERN EVALUATION

The final selection is an evaluation of indentured servitude by a twentieth-century writer. ☐ Abbot Emerson Smith, *White Servitude and Convict Labor in America, 1607–1776,* pp. 305–306. Chapel Hill: University of North Carolina Press. Copyright © 1947.

It is worth asking whether this system was necessary, and whether a less burdensome method might not have been devised. One can easily invent schemes of colonization much more pleasant than that actually used; plenty of people did so in those days and have done so since. But the practical difficulty with all these schemes was that they were much too expensive, considered in relation to the wealth of society generally. A plan which worked well in the nineteenth century could not have been financed in the seventeenth or eighteenth. Thus, theoretically, the original project of the Virginia Company was more generous and equitable than the individualistic system of white servitude, but it did not work because it was too expensive for the time. The most attractive schemes actually carried out were those of Georgia and Halifax, where men were transported, fed and sheltered for a year, and then turned loose with a grant of land to fend for themselves. But these again were both very costly; small as they were they strained the available resources which the British Treasury itself could devote to them. One is forced to the conclusion that if colonization was to be carried on at all, the only way to do it without rearranging society in some utopian fashion was to set up the system of indentured white labor. This does not, of course, mean that masters had to be cruel, that servants had to be kidnapped, or even that they had to serve for as long a time as four years. Many details could have been improved, but generally considered the system was sound and well adapted to the practical necessities of the situation, both for servants and for masters.

Essentially it was simply a workable means of supplying white settlers and cheap labor. Its social consequences were by no means altogether good . . . . Perhaps it was a fortunate thing that pioneer conditions were as difficult as they were, if there is any truth in theories of heredity, for the weak, diseased, and unenterprising were not preserved. The strong and competent survived, and if this manner of separating sheep from goats put too great a premium on sheer physical health, that at least was something well worth distinguishing and preserving. . . . [The] residue, such as it was, became the American people.

PROBLEM 2

Craftsmen and the Courts

One of the most important economic developments in the United States from 1790 to 1840 was the change in emphasis from custom-made goods to the production of standardized items for a wider national market. Improvements in manufacture, transportation, and merchandising techniques brought an increasing volume of products to retail and wholesale dealers. This, in turn, drastically changed the status of the independent craftsman and of the journeyman who worked for him.

The sale of goods to dealers, rather than directly to consumers, resulted in increased competition. In order to capture a larger share of the market, manufacturers often cut their prices. Although part of this loss was offset by increased sales, employers also cut the wages of workingmen to maintain what they considered an adequate profit margin.

In order to bring pressure on employers to maintain or raise wages, journeymen organized craft associations. Such combinations of workingmen were considered illegal according to the common-law doctrine, recognized by the courts, which regarded labor organizations as conspiracies. Organizing an association or participating in a strike often resulted in fines and other punishment for the workers.

In the early nineteenth century most Americans would have agreed that a combination of workers was undesirable and potentially injurious to both the public and the employer. It was commonly held that successful strikes led to higher prices and therefore harmed the consumer. Strikes were thought to harm an employer by making it difficult for him to compete with other owners who continued to pay workers a lower wage.

Many Americans of the early nineteenth century viewed with suspicion any collective action on the part of workmen because it seemed to be a threat against individual freedom. Compelling a worker to join a union or participate in a strike seemed to be an invasion of his rights. Although many reasons such as these were advanced in opposition to unions, the basic motive of the employer was to prevent an increase in wages. This objection, however, was not the one usually stressed.

The court cases which resulted from this interaction of workers and employers provoked considerable discussion and raised many questions which are still being debated today. Many of the issues have to do with the desirability of the closed shop (a provision that only union workers may be employed), the effect of strikes on the national welfare, and the role of government in labor disputes, as well as others which are discussed in the following readings. Consider these questions as you read:

1 What are the major issues at stake in the case of the Philadelphia Cordwainers? Do the defense and the prosecution stress the same matters?

2 What seems to be the major objective of the prosecution in the Philadelphia Cordwainers case? What activities of workers' organizations did the prosecution most oppose? Why?

3 After reading the excerpts from the constitution of the Journeymen Cordwainers of the City of New York, what do you consider to be the primary goal of the organization?

4 What is the position which Chief Justice Shaw took about the legality of unions in *Commonwealth* v. *Hunt*? How did his position differ from that of the prosecution in the Philadelphia Cordwainers case?

I

THE CASE OF THE PHILADELPHIA CORDWAINERS

In the case of *Commonwealth* v. *Pullis,* the Philadelphia Cordwainers (boot and shoemakers) were brought to trial in 1806, charged with criminal conspiracy. The indictment included charges that association members conspired to raise wages, refused to work for an employer who paid less than a fixed rate, and prevented workers who were not members of the association from being hired. Defendants were found guilty and each fined $8.00 plus costs. The first selection that follows is from the defense attorney's final appeal to the jury. ☐ John R. Commons, editor, *A Documentary History of American Industrial Society*, Vol. 3, pp. 163, 170, 171–172, 196–197, 198–199. Cleveland: The Arthur H. Clark Company, copyright © 1910.

[The] real question now at issue, between the state and the defendants . . . is nothing more or less than this, whether the wealthy master shoemakers of this populous and flourishing city, shall charge you and me what price they please for our boots and shoes, and at the same time have the privilege of fixing the wages of the poor journeymen they happen to employ. . . .

. . . When I hear men who have inherited large fortunes from their ancestors, or to use a familiar expression, have been born with silver spoons in their mouths, advocating distinctions in society, and espousing measures calculated to affect and oppress the labouring classes of the community, I feel a degree of charity for the errors they commit, because they have been taught from infancy to exercise an overbearing, insulting superiority over those who really are their equals. They fancy that there is some inherent quality in themselves, which entitles them to rank and precedence above the common herd. . . .

. . . If it be true, as they have contended, that the best, and fastest workers among the journeymen, by toiling at the last, late and early, can earn twelve dollars a week, I think it has been satisfactorily proved, that the masters receive a clear nett profit deducting the expence of materials, equal to the amount of wages which they pay their journeymen. From this, it must evidently appear, that those who employ twenty-four journeymen, must make near fifteen thousand dollars a year, when the best journeyman receives about six hundred, a sum scarcely adequate to the frugal maintenance of himself and his family in this city, tho' living on the simplest and cheapest fare which the market affords. Why then, in the name of common sense, are they charged with avarice and extortion? The labourer is surely worthy of sufficient hire to enable him to live comfortably. . . .

. . . [There] is no legislative scale established, by which the wages of journeymen of any description are graduated and adjusted. . . . We have pursued an object, not contravening any positive provision, nor contrary to the established principles of the common law, and we must be innocent.

The determination of any number, not to lodge in the same boarding house with particular individuals, surely cannot be considered as a confederation wrongfully to injure them, let it proceed from whim, caprice, or any other motive. The old proverb says, a man is known by the company he keeps; and you must permit every body to choose their associates. Should you establish the contrary principle by your verdict, I beg you to contemplate the consequences. The masters, I suppose, will then select at pleasure the houses in which we must board. They may order us to lodge in the hospital or the bettering house, if they will receive us. If you give them the right to choose where we shall live, they will have equal authority to say how. They may fix our diet, and declare, whether we shall dine on turtle soup and roast beef, or on barley broth and the legs of frogs. . . .

. . . If you banish from this place, (as it is morally certain you will,) a great number of the best workmen, by a verdict of guilty, can you reasonably expect, that labour will be cheaper? Will it not rise in value, in exact proportion to the scarcity of hands, and the demand for boots and shoes, like every other article in the market? My learned friend has said, he was advocating the interests of the journeymen, I assert, that when rationally understood, I am pleading the cause of the masters. Remember I now tell you, that if you convict the defendants, for asking the same wages which are received in New-York and Baltimore; not a month will elapse, before the present prosecutors will gladly offer them the same terms, and they will entreat those they have driven away, to return and work for them. If you will take my advice, you will leave the regulation of these things to the open market. There every article, like water, acquires its natural level: adopt this rule, and you will be more likely to get your boots much cheaper.

The prosecuting attorney stated his case as follows. ☐ *A Documentary History of American Industrial Society,* Vol. 3, pp. 206–207, 208–209, 218–219, 220, 221.

I say, that clubs and self-constituted societies are legal, useful, and proper to be encouraged; you cannot reach the defendants on that ground, for my part I will not attempt it.

If, however, they usurp power, abridge the rights of others to extend their own, it is an aristocracy not the less detestable, that it moves in a small sphere. . . .

The defendants formed a society, the object of which was . . . What? That they should not be obliged to work for wages which they did not think a reasonable compensation? No: If that was the sole object of the society, I approve it. . . . No man is to work without a reasonable compensation: they may legally and properly associate for that purpose. . . . If they go beyond this, and say we will not work, but we will compel the employers to give more, not according to contract, but such as they separately think themselves entitled to receive. . . .

The first feature of compulsion in this society, to compel the employers to give the wages they demand . . . is, that strangers are forced to join their body on the penalty of embarrassment, and being denied the means of earning their own support . . . the members are denied the liberty of separating, and their rules are inforced by pains, penalties, and fines; threats, and even violence. . . . I have no hostility against these men, they are a valuable and useful part of the community; they ought to be, and will be encouraged and protected. I make no attempts to take away their rights, I only say they must not trespass on the rights of their employers.

I shall, for perspicuity sake, class my observations under two heads. First, whether any conspiracy exists, and what is its object, nature, and extent? Second, What part have the defendants, according to the evidence, taken in carrying into execution such combination?

In the first place, what is this society, so terrible in its effects, so secret in its formation, and which exercises an authority which the legislature could not confer? . . . I take the representation of their own leading witness . . . James Keagan said, . . . "that if a journeyman comes here from a neighbouring state, or Europe, we insist that he shall join our society." He goes on and states, "or we will neither work, nor suffer any of the society to work with him in any shop where he is employed, until he is turned away." And that the society is to fix the rate of wages, and whoever deviates from the rule prescribed, is liable to all the penal consequences as if he never had been a member.

Now, what is the complaint? Last October or November, in conformity with this article of the constitution, they entered into an agreement to obtain an advance of wages, and to punish, as heretofore stated, all who shall contravene this regulation. . . . I pause to consider, whether the combination I have stated is lawful. . . .

Their measures are said to be not compulsive; what then are they? Recollect the circumstance . . . Mr. Bedford is notified, "you have scabs in your shop, turn them off, or" . . . Well, he neglects to comply: . . . the shop is scabbed: he is left without his journeymen: in a great proportion, ruin awaits him: he talks of investing his capital in the dry good business. I shall be driven from the city, he tells the witness, if this continues; and concludes with an honourable declaration—at all events, I will not discharge you let the consequences be what they may; while you do your duty, we will sink or swim together! . . .

They say, no force was employed—Force, yes, they threw a potato through the window which passed near his face, and that the author of the malicious injury might be known, it contains the ends of half a dozen broken shoe-maker's tacks. . . .

Mr. Franklin told you this was a cause of importance; it is eminently so; and it depends on your verdict, whether this manufacture shall flourish or decay. These defendants call on an employer, Mr. Montgomery . . . . They demanded certain wages, and asked whether the employer would or would not give them? and added, "if they will not we will take means to make them."

. . . Have the citizens of Philadelphia imposed upon the employers the duty of paying the wages demanded by the defendants? We claim no immemorial custom: we say it is a matter of contract, neither employers or journeymen have a right to insist, or the other shall pay or receive a rate of wages, to which they have not freely consented. . . .

. . . We charge a combination, by means of rewards and punishments, threats, insults, starvings and beatings, to compel the employers to accede to terms, they the journeymen present and dictate. If the journeymen cordwainers may do this, so may the employers; the carpenters, brick-layers, butchers, farmers, and the whole community will be formed into hostile confederacies, the prelude and certain forefunner of bloodshed and civil war.

II

CONSTITUTION OF AN EARLY LABOR UNION

In a case against the Journeymen Cordwainers of the City of New York, in 1810, the constitution of the organization was used by the prosecution as evidence. Pertinent sections of the document are presented below. ⟧ *A Documentary History of American Industrial Society,* Vol. 3, pp. 364–365, 366, 367.

We, the Journeymen Cordwainers of the City of New-York, impressed with a sense of our just rights, and to guard against the intrigues or artifices that may at any time be used by our employers to reduce our wages lower than what we deem an adequate reward for our labour, have unanimously agreed to the following articles as the Constitution of our Society. . . .

ARTICLE III. The President, in order to preserve regularity and decorum, is authorized to fine any member six cents, that is not silent, when order is called for by him, and all members are to address the chair, one at a time.

ARTICLE IV. Any person becoming a member of this Society, shall pay the sum of forty-three and a half cents on his admission, and six and a quarter cents as his monthly contribution; . . . and should any member, leave the city at any time, and stay for the space of three months or upwards, if on his return it can be proved that he has been so absent, he shall still be deemed a lawful member, by paying one month's contribution. . . .

ARTICLE VIII. No member of this society shall work for an employer, that has any Journeyman Cordwainer, or his apprentice in his employment, that does not belong to this Society, unless the Journeyman come and join the same; and should any . . . member work on the seat with any person or persons that has not joined this society, and do not report the same to the President, the first meeting night after it comes to his knowledge, shall pay a fine of one dollar.

ARTICLE IX. If any employer should reduce his Journeyman's wages at any time, or should the said Journeyman find himself otherwise aggrieved, by reporting the same to the Committee at their next meeting, they shall lay the case before the society, who shall determine on what measures to take to redress the same.

ARTICLE X. The name of each member shall be regularly called over at every monthly meeting, and should any member be absent when his name has been called over three times successively, shall pay a fine of twelve and a half cents for the first night, twenty-five cents for the second, and fifty cents for the third; and if absent three successive meeting nights, the Secretary shall deliver him a notice, and if he does not make his appearance after being notified, on the following meeting night, (unless he can assign some just cause for staying away,) shall pay a fine of three dollars.

ARTICLE XI. Any Journeyman Cordwainer, coming into this city, that does not come forward and join this society in the space of one month, (as soon as it is known,) he shall be notified by the Secretary, and for such notification he shall pay twelve and a half cents; and if he does not come forward and join the same on the second meeting of the society, after receiving the notice, shall pay a fine of three dollars.

ARTICLE XII. Any member of this society having an apprentice or apprentices, shall, when he or they become free, report the . . . same to the President, on the first monthly meeting following; and if the said apprentice or apprentices do not come forward and join the Society in the space of one month from the time of report, shall be notified by the Secretary, and if he does not come forward within two months after receiving the notification, shall pay a fine of three dollars. . . .

ARTICLE XIV. If any member should be guilty of giving a brother member any abusive language in the society-room, during the hours of meeting, who might have been excluded from this society by his misdemeanor, but by making concession have been reunited, he shall pay a fine of twenty-five cents.

III

A CASE FOR LABOR

One of the most significant decisions in the history of American labor came in the Massachusetts case of *Commonwealth* v. *Hunt,* in which Chief Justice Lemuel Shaw rendered the decision. Excerpts from this decision follow. Although his ruling upheld the legality of trade unions and strikes for a closed shop, it is important to note that union activity was still subject to attacks in the courts. □   4 Metcalf 111 (Massachusetts, 1842).

Stripped . . . of . . . introductory recitals and alleged injurious consequences, and of the qualifying epithets attached to the facts, the averment is this; that the defendants and others formed themselves into a society, and agreed not to work for any person, who should employ any journeyman or other person, not a member of such society, after notice given him to discharge such workman.

The manifest intent of the association is, to induce all those engaged in the same occupation to become members of it. Such a purpose is not unlawful. It would give them a power which might be exerted for useful and honorable purposes, or for dangerous and pernicious ones. If the latter were the real and actual object, and susceptible of proof, it should have been specially charged. Such an association might be used to afford each other assistance in times of poverty, sickness and distress; or to raise their intellectual, moral and social condition; or to make improvement in their art; or for other proper purposes. Or the association might be designed for purposes of oppression and injustice. But in order to charge all those, who become members of an association, with the guilt of a criminal conspiracy, it must be . . . proved that the actual, if not the avowed object of the association, was criminal. . . . The law is not to be hoodwinked by colorable pretences. It looks at truth and reality, through whatever disguise it may assume. . . . In this case, no such secret agreement, varying the objects of the association from those avowed, is set forth in this count of the indictment. . . .

. . . The case supposes that these persons are not bound by contract, but free to work for whom they please, or not to work, if they so prefer. In this state of things, we cannot perceive, that it is criminal for men to agree together to exercise their own acknowledged rights, in such a manner as best to subserve their own interests. . . .

. . . It is perfectly consistent with every thing stated in this count, that the effect of the agreement was, that when they were free to act, they would not engage with an employer, or continue in his employment, if such employer, when free to act, should engage with a workman, or continue a workman in his employment, not a member of the association. If a large number of men, engaged for a certain time, should combine together to violate their contract, and quit their employment together, it would present a very different question. . . .

The second count . . . alleges that the defendants, with others unknown, did assemble, conspire, confederate and agree together, not to work for any master or person who should employ any workman not being a member of a certain club, society or combination, called the Boston Journeymen Bootmakers' Society . . . and that by means of said conspiracy they did compel one Isaac B. Wait, a master cordwainer, to turn out of his employ one Jeremiah Horne, a journeyman boot-maker . . . . So far as the . . . conspiracy is concerned, all the remarks made in reference to the first count are equally applicable to this. It is simply an . . . agreement amongst themselves not to work for a person, who should employ any person not a member of a certain association. It sets forth no illegal or criminal purpose to be accomplished, nor any illegal or criminal means to be adopted for the accomplishment of any purpose. It was an agreement, as to the manner in which they would exercise an acknowledged right to contract with others for their labor. It does not aver a conspiracy or even an intention to raise their wages . . . .

. . . If . . . the indictment had averred a conspiracy, by the defendants, to compel Wait to turn Horne out of his employment, and to accomplish that object by the use of force or fraud, it would have been a very different case; especially if . . . Wait was under obligation, by contract, for an unexpired term of time, to employ and pay Horne. As before remarked, it would have been a conspiracy to do an unlawful, though not a criminal act, to induce Wait to violate his engagement, to the actual injury of Horne. . . . [Every] free man, whether skilled laborer, mechanic, farmer or domestic servant, may work or not work, or work or refuse to work with any company or individual, at his own option except so far as he is bound by contract. . . . It was the agreement not to work for him, by which they compelled Wait to decline employing Horne longer. . . .

If the fact of depriving Jeremiah Horne of the profits of his business, by whatever means it might be done, would be unlawful and criminal, a combination to compass that object would be an unlawful conspiracy, and it would be unnecessary to state the means. . . .

Suppose a baker in a small village had the exclusive custom of his neighborhood, and was making large profits by the sale of his bread. Supposing a number of those neighbors, believing the price of his bread too high, should propose to him to reduce his prices, or if he did not, that they would introduce another baker; and on his refusal, such other baker should, under their encouragement, set up a rival establishment, and sell his bread at lower prices; the effect would be to diminish the profit of the former baker, and to the same extent to impoverish him. And it might be said and proved, that the purpose of the associates was to diminish his profits, and thus impoverish him, though the ultimate and laudable object of the combination was to reduce the cost of bread to themselves and their neighbors. The same thing may be said of all competition in every branch of trade and industry; and yet it is through that competition, that the best interests of trade and industry are promoted. . . .

We think, therefore, that associations may be entered into, the object of which is to adopt measures that may have a tendency to impoverish another, that is, to diminish his gains and profits, and yet so far from being criminal or unlawful, the object may be highly meritorious and public spirited. The legality of such an association will therefore depend upon the means to be used for its accomplishment. If it is to be carried into effect by fair or honorable and lawful means, it is, to say the least, innocent; if by falsehood or force, it may be stamped with the character of conspiracy. . . .

It appears . . . that it was contended on the part of the defendants, that this indictment did not set forth any agreement to do a criminal act, or to do any lawful act by criminal means, and that the agreement therein set forth did not constitute a conspiracy indictable by the law of this State, and that the court was requested so to instruct the jury. This the court declined doing, but instructed the jury . . . that the society, organized and associated for the purposes described in the indictment, was an unlawful conspiracy against the laws of this State, and that if the jury believed, from the evidence, that the defendants or any of them had engaged in such confederacy, they were bound to find such of them guilty.

In this opinion of the learned judge, this court, for the reasons stated, cannot concur. Whatever illegal purpose can be found in the constitution of the Bootmakers' Society, it not being clearly set forth in the indictment, cannot be relied upon to support this conviction. . . . [We] cannot perceive that it charges a criminal conspiracy punishable by law. The exceptions must, therefore, be sustained, and the judgment arrested.

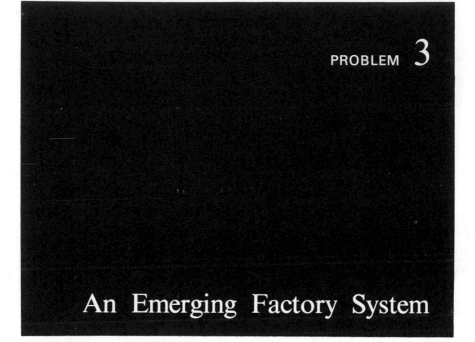

PROBLEM 3

An Emerging Factory System

The beginnings of the factory system became evident in the United States during the first half of the nineteenth century. At first, factories were concentrated in the textile industry, where power-driven machinery quickly transformed methods of production. A new type of labor force, composed mainly of young women recruited from the farms, emerged to run the new machines. In some areas entire families moved from farm to factory town to tend the looms and spindles.

Many vexing problems became apparent as the factory system changed American economic life. Conditions of work were very different from those which had prevailed in the era of handicraft. Workers recruited from farms had to be disciplined to the requirements of the machine. In Europe and in England the growth of industry had created working conditions which were already a festering source of social unrest. A similar development began to affect the United States.

In the New England region a unique arrangement called the Lowell System offered a temporary answer to the problem of supplying an industrial labor force. The first two readings of Problem 3 concern this unusual development which combined commercialism with a paternalistic regard for the welfare of the workers. The Lowell System was confined to a few industries in New England, however. Most of the workers elsewhere in the United States during this period labored under quite different conditions.

Around the middle of the nineteenth century, the arrival of thousands of immigrants complicated the labor problem. The great potato famines in Ireland and in the Rhineland sent hosts of Irish and European farmers to American shores. Employers welcomed this fresh supply of willing hands. But as immigrant and native worker began to compete, a number of conflicts broke out. These conflicts were soon reflected in the resolutions of labor organizations and the platforms of political parties.

The selections which follow attempt to focus attention on some of the most significant aspects of problems arising from the emergence of an American industrial society. As you read, keep in mind the following questions:

1 How do you account for the differences in opinion between Buckingham and the writer of the article from *The Harbinger?* What standards did each writer use as a basis for his judgment?

2 "The far greater number of fortunes, accumulated by the North in comparison with the South, shows that hireling labor is more profitable for Capital than slave labor." Is this statement from *The Harbinger* valid?

3 Can you draw any conclusions about the reliability of the third selection from the tone of the writer?

4 According to the final selection, why did industrialists try to attract foreign labor? Would you agree with the writer's description of foreign workers?

5 How were the problems facing factory workers similar to and different from those facing hand craftsmen? Why did trade unions first emerge among the craftsmen?

I

A FOREIGNER'S VIEW OF THE LOWELL FACTORIES

The first selection is an account of life and working conditions in the Lowell, Massachusetts, textile mills during the 1830's. The writer, James S. Buckingham, an Englishman, traveled extensively throughout Europe and America during this period. □ James S. Buckingham, *The Eastern and Western States of America*, Vol. 1, pp. 296–301. London: Fisher, Son & Co., 1842.

All the men that I saw employed in either of these works were better dressed, cleaner, and appeared better fed, healthier, and more contented, than the same class of persons in England; and they have good reason to be so, as they are better paid, earning from 6 to 12 dollars per week, and some of the more skilful 15 dollars—with less cost for living, the enjoyment of all political rights, and the power at any time to emigrate to the West at little charge, whenever their wages should be in danger of being reduced. All the females that we saw—and they exceeded 3,000—were still more superior to the same class of persons in England. They were all remarkably clean, well-dressed, and supplied with requisites for warmth and comfort. The windows of the room in which they worked were curtained towards the south; and in every window-seat or sill were seen exotic or native shrubs, plants, and flowers, in neatly-made flower-boxes or baskets, painted green, belonging to these young females; who cultivate them as pets or favourites, in their leisure moments, and watch their growth, their health, and their flowering, with as much interest as any lady in Christendom. These, too, had the air of being more happy than the factory-girls, as a class, in England; and they have abundant reasons for being so, from the actual superiority of their condition; for they earn more wages, have better food and clothing, work in greater comfort, lay by more money, and rarely enter upon the occupation till 14 or 15, and generally leave it before they are 20.

The greater number of the females employed here, are daughters of the farmers in the three States of Massachusetts, New Hampshire, and Vermont. They do not leave their homes from want, but from a love of independence, and a desire to support themselves by their own labour. They therefore rarely come to the factories till they are 15 or 16; and there is a law prohibiting their being employed before they are 14, unless on the condition of their being at school at least three months in the year. When they come, they are in general amply provided with clothes, and every other requisite; and from the first day, they are comfortably accommodated in one of the boarding-houses belonging to the Company in whose factory they may be employed to work. These boarding-houses are neat dwellings, of brick or wood, two and three stories high, built in streets and rows, by the respective Companies, for their own operatives only. They are let at a rent which yields only 5 per cent. interest on their cost, (though 10 per cent. is the lowest profit on their working capital,) to matrons chosen by the Company, and under their control, as well as responsible to the Directors for the adoption and enforcement of such regulations as they may propose. These matrons are bound to furnish a prescribed number of meals, with regulated quantities and qualities of the articles to the young boarders, at fixed rates; so that there shall be no misunderstanding on either side. The number of boarders that may be taken by each matron, who are mostly widows, is also limited; and no other persons than those actually employed in the factory to which the boarding-house belongs, are permitted to be taken in or entertained at the house, nor are any males admitted among the female boarders there.

Among the regulations by which these establishments are governed, the following deserve mention: 1. Good behaviour in words and actions, and the constant observance of temperance and virtue, are the duties exacted from all, whether in the factory or the boarding-house, as well as diligence and subordination; and any person violating any of the rules and regulations of either branch, are to be punished with instant dismissal. 2. No ardent spirits or intoxicating drinks of any kind are allowed to be used or possessed by any persons, of either sex—agent, overseer, or operative. 3. No games of chance or hazard, such as cards, dice, or backgammon, are at any time allowed. 4. Every person employed must live in one of the boarding-houses, subject to the Company's rules; and all who are not prevented by sickness, must attend divine worship, at such church as they prefer, and rigidly respect the sanctity of the Sabbath. 5. The doors of every boarding-house must be closed at 10 o'clock at night; and no relaxation of this rule to be admitted on any occasion. 6. A report must be made of the misconduct of any individual guilty of a breach of any of these rules by the matron of the boarding house, to the Directors of the Company. . . .

The hours of work are from 6 in the morning to 7 in the evening in the summer; and from half-past 6 to half-past 7 in the winter months, with the allowance of one hour to the two meals of breakfast at 8 and dinner at 1 o'clock, supper being taken after their labours are over. On Saturdays the factories are closed at 4 o'clock, so that the labour is 12 hours a day on each day except Saturday, and then only 9. This is no doubt longer than it is desirable that *any* person should labour continuously, more especially young persons, and still more especially females: but I have no doubt, that from the superior cleanliness, comfort, food, air, and healthful associations by which they are surrounded, their 12 hours' labour here do not produce more fatigue to them, than 10 hours' labour do to the same class of factory-girls in England. But even this is too much; and since it is certain, that, by the great improvements in machinery, one pair of hands can now perform as much as fifty pair of hands could do but a few years since, there *ought* to be an abridgment of the labour performed by the operative classes, as the consequence of such improvements; and in a justly-regulated state of society, where labour should have its full share of profit as well as capital, it *would* be so—though whether the world is making any nearer approach to such a state of things, seems at least very doubtful. What makes this amount of labour more easily borne, however, by the factory operatives here, than it is by their less fortunate sisterhood in England, is this—that none of them consider it as their permanent condition; all look forward to its termination in a few years at the farthest; and every one must be aware of how much greater a burden can be borne, under the confident hope of its soon ceasing, than could possibly be endured, if the sufferers thought it would last for ever. The men earn here from 12 to 20 dollars a week, and can therefore lay by from 5 to 10 dollars, after providing for every want, so that in two or three years they accumulate enough to go off to the West, and buy an estate at 1¼ dollar an acre, or set up in some small way of business at home. The girls earn from 3 to 5 dollars per week, and the cost of their board being fixed at 1¼ dollars per week, they can lay by, after paying for everything needed, from 1 to 3 dollars per week; and thus in three or four years, they may return home to their father's house with a little capital of from 200 to 300 dollars, and marry advantageously to some young farmer, or other person of their own rank in life. This is sometimes but not often done before they have finished their term of service in the factory; in which case, the female invariably leaves that occupation, and remains at home, nor ever returns to the factory, unless early widowhood and the death of parents should render such a step necessary. The proportion of married women to single employed in these works, is not more than 1 in 100, of those whose husbands are alive; and of widows, about 2 in 100 of the whole number.

II

LOWELL THROUGH OTHER EYES

The same factories are described in an early American labor publication, *The Harbinger,* of November 14, 1846. ☐ John R. Commons, editor, *A Documentary History of American Industrial Society,* Vol. 7, pp. 132–135. Cleveland: The Arthur H. Clark Company, copyright © 1910.

We have lately visited the cities of Lowell and Manchester, and have had an opportunity of examining the factory system more closely than before. We had distrusted the accounts, which we had heard from persons engaged in the Labor Reform, now beginning to agitate New England; we could scarcely credit the statements made in relation to the exhausting nature of the labor in the mills, and to the manner in which the young women, the operatives, lived in their boarding-houses, six sleeping in a room, poorly ventilated.

We went through many of the mills, talked particularly to a large number of the operatives, and ate at their boarding-houses, on purpose to ascertain by personal inspection the facts of the case. We assure our readers that very little information is possessed, and no correct judgments formed, by the public at large, of our factory system, which is the first germ of the Industrial or Commercial Feudalism, that is to spread over our land. . . .

In Lowell live between seven and eight thousand young women, who are generally daughters of farmers of the different States of New England; some of them are members of families that were rich the generation before. . . .

The operatives work thirteen hours a day in the summer time, and from daylight to dark in the winter. At half past four in the morning the factory bell rings, and at five the girls must be in the mills. A clerk, placed as a watch, observes those who are a few minutes behind the time, and effectual means are taken to stimulate to punctuality. This is the morning commencement of the industrial discipline—(should we not rather say industrial tyranny?) which is established in these Associations of this moral and Christian community. At seven the girls are allowed thirty minutes for breakfast, and at noon thirty minutes more for dinner, except during the first quarter of the year, when the time is extended to forty-five minutes. But within this time they must hurry to their boarding-houses and return to the factory, and that through the hot sun, or the rain and cold. A meal eaten under such circumstances must be quite unfavorable to digestion and health, as any medical man will inform us. At seven o'clock in the evening the factory bell sounds the close of the day's work.

Thus thirteen hours per day of close attention and monotonous labor are exacted from the young women in these manufactories. . . . So fatigued—we should say, exhausted and worn out, but we wish to speak of the system in the simplest language—are numbers of the girls, that they go to bed soon after their evening meal, and endeavor by a comparatively long sleep to resuscitate their weakened frames for the toils of the coming day. When Capital has got thirteen hours of labor daily out of a being, it can get nothing more. It would be a poor speculation in an industrial point of view to own the operative; for the trouble and expense of providing for times of sickness and old age would more than counterbalance the difference between the price of wages and the expense of board and clothing. The far greater number of fortunes, accumulated by the North in comparison with the South, shows that hireling labor is more profitable for Capital than slave labor.

Now let us examine the nature of the labor itself, and the conditions under which it is performed. Enter with us into the large rooms, when the looms are at work. The largest that we saw is in the Amoskeag Mills at Manchester. It is four hundred feet long, and about seventy broad; there are five hundred looms, and twenty-one thousand spindles in it. The din and clatter of these five hundred looms under full operation, struck us on first entering as something frightful and infernal, for it seemed such an atrocious violation of one of the faculties of the human soul, the sense of hearing. After a while we became somewhat inured to it, and by speaking quite close to the ear of an operative and quite loud, we could hold a conversation . . . .

The girls attend upon an average three looms; many attend four, but this requires a very active person, and the most unremitting care. However, a great many do it. Attention to two is as much as should be demanded of an operative. This gives us some idea of the application required during the thirteen hours of daily labor. The atmosphere of such a room cannot of course be pure; on the contrary it is charged with cotton filaments and dust, which, we were told, are very injurious to the lungs. On entering the room, although the day was warm, we remarked that the windows were down; we asked the reason, and a young woman answered very naïvely, and without seeming to be in the least aware that this privation of fresh air was anything else than perfectly natural, that "when the wind blew, the threads did not work so well." . . .

The young women sleep upon an average six in a room; three beds to a room. There is no privacy, no retirement here; it is almost impossible to read or write alone, as the parlor is full and so many sleep in the same chamber. A young woman remarked to us, that if she had a letter to write, she did it on the head of a band-box, sitting on a trunk, as there was not space for a table. So live and toil the young women of our country in the boarding-houses and manufactories, which the rich . . . have built for them.

III

GATHERING THE WORKERS

Problems of recruiting workers for the mills of New England continued to plague employers, who sometimes resorted to drastic methods. The following selection describes one system of obtaining workers. ☐ *A Documentary History of American Industrial Society*, Vol. 3, p. 141.

We were not aware until within a few days, of the *modus operandi* of the Factory powers in this village, of forcing poor girls from their quiet homes, to become their tools, and like the southern slaves, to give up her life and liberty to the heartless tyrants and task-masters. Observing a singular looking, "long, low, black" wagon passing along the street, we made inquiries respecting it, and were informed that it was what we term "a slaver." She makes regular trips to the north of the state, cruising around in Vermont and New Hampshire, with a "commander" whose heart must be as black as his craft, who is paid a dollar a head, for all he brings to the market, and more in proportion to the distance—If they bring them from such a distance that they cannot easily get back. This is done by "hoisting false colors," and representing to the girls, that they can tend more machinery than is possible, and that the work is so very neat, and the wages such, that they can dress in silks and spend half their time in reading. Now, is this true? Let those girls who have been thus deceived, answer.

Let us say a word in regard to the manner in which they are stowed, in the wagon, which may find a similarity only in the manner in which slaves are fastened in the hold of a vessel. It is long, and the seats so close that it must be very inconvenient. Is there any humanity in this? Philanthropists may talk of negro slavery, but it would be well first to endeavor to emancipate the slaves at home. Let us not stretch our ears to catch the sound of the lash on the flesh of the oppressed black while the oppressed in our very midst are crying out in thunder tones, and calling upon us for assistance.

Rosy pictures of employment opportunities in the United States were also spread throughout Europe. Descriptions such as the following from a popular emigrants' guide helped to attract thousands of newcomers. □ S. H. Collins, *The Emigrants' Guide to the United States of America,* pp. 52–53. Boston: Joseph Noble, 1829.

Industrious men need never lack employment in America; labourers, carpenters, masons, bricklayers, stone cutters, blacksmiths, tanners, weavers, farriers, carriers, tailors and shoe makers, and all useful mechanics are sure of work and wages—artizans receive better pay than in Europe, and they can live with less exertion and more comfort.

From what I have seen of America, east of the Alleghany mountains, I judge that artizans in general will succeed in any part; and that labourers of all sorts will greatly improve their condition; they will, if saving and industrious, soon acquire enough to enable them to migrate further in quest of land, on which they may become proprietors.

It is not every emigrant who succeeds: no, it is only the sober, the honest, and industrious; happy those to whom the transition has proven a powerful spur to prosperity; and to the good establishment of children born in the days of their poverty, and who had no other position to expect than the rags of their parents, had it not been for their happy emigration. . . .

Any one in any vocation, manual or mechanical, may, by honest industry and ordinary prudence, acquire an independent provision for himself and family; so high are the wages of labour, averaging at least double the rate in England, and quadruple that of France; so comparatively scanty the population, so great the demand for all kinds of work.

IV

PLEA OF THE NATIVIST

Demands for restriction of immigration became more and more insistent as foreign workers poured into the country from 1846 to 1855. American workingmen, through their associations, were especially active in this protest, as indicated in the following excerpt from a labor journal. □ *A Documentary History of American Industrial Society,* Vol. 3, p. 89.

Now the capitalists of the Danville Iron works wish to protect themselves against these "disorderly strikes," by importing a surplus of help; the Lowell capitalists entertain the same republican idea of self protection, the Pittsburg and Alleghany city capitalists, whose sympathies, (if they have any,) have been recently appealed to, wish to secure themselves against "turn-outs" by creating a numerous poor and dependant populace. Isolated capital everywhere and in all ages protects itself by the poverty ignorance and servility of a surplus population, who will submit to its base requirements—hence the democratic or whig capital of the United States is striving to fill the country with foreign workmen—English workmen, whose abject condition in their own country has made them tame, submissive and "peaceable, orderly citizens;" that is, work fourteen and sixteen hours per day, for what capital sees fit to give them, and if it is not enough to provide them a comfortable house to shelter their wives and children and furnish them with decent food and clothes, why, they must live in cellars, go hungry and ragged!—and for this state of things, capitalists are not answerable. O! no—"they (the laborers) aint obliged to take it—they are free to go when they please!"

Workingmen in the Era of Jackson

The expansion of the American economy during the first half of the nine-teenth century occurred during a period when equally momentous develop-ments appeared in the political system. Especially during the period of Jacksonian Democracy, the newly won political power of the common man was directed toward the improvement of his lot in many areas. The reform movements of the time were concerned with a great variety of political, economic, and social issues.

To students of the contemporary American labor movement, some of the demands of union members of the 1830's seem quite unusual. They demanded broadening of the free public school system and elimination of the practice of imprisonment for debts. They wanted changes in the court and jury system, regulation of banking, abolition of state laws requiring attendance at militia drills, extension of civil rights, and liberalization of election laws. None of these reforms would have brought direct economic benefits to the workers. Moreover, they were designed for the general betterment of society rather than for the aid of specific groups of workers.

Why should union members have concentrated so much of their attention upon political matters of general concern to society? Why not instead try to obtain higher wages and better working conditions through striking against particular employers? Perhaps the answers to these two questions lie in the backgrounds of the union leaders and the laws regulating labor during this period.

Many union leaders were not factory workers and had not yet accepted the fact that such workers' lives would be spent permanently within the walls of a mill. Furthermore, conspiracy regulations made striking a dangerous tactic to employ.

Universal manhood suffrage became an established fact in practically all of the states by 1830. As the enfranchised workingman turned to political action, it was logical that he should look for an organization to represent his causes. At first many "workingmen's parties" appeared. Typical of minor and third parties in American history, these organizations waxed and waned, their programs finally being absorbed by the major political groups.

The death of these minor parties did not lessen the demand for reform. The growing role of labor in the United States was reflected in the remarkable growth of unions during the four years that preceded the Panic of 1837.

Organized labor successfully courted both skilled and unskilled workers. Most major cities had a "trade union" organization designed to promote mutual strike assistance and to lobby, or exert pressures, in state and national legislatures. In 1835 these groups joined together to form the National Trades Union, which enjoyed a short-lived success. The economic collapse of 1837 destroyed the movement.

The readings in this Problem illustrate the varied interests and aims of this early attempt at trade unionism. Consider the following questions as you read:

1 What do the goals of the New York Workingman's party reveal about the objectives of workingmen during the period? Do these men seem to have accepted permanently their position as wage earners?

2 Why should workingmen of the period place such stress on the importance of free public education?

3 What were the major arguments of the building-trades workers in Boston in favor of the ten-hour day? How did the workers hope to win shorter hours?

4 What place of importance would you assign to the question of banks in the listing of labor's grievances? Why?

5 Why should labor during this period turn to political rather than to economic action?

I

AIMS OF A WORKINGMAN'S PARTY

The diversity of the goals of labor during the Jacksonian period is revealed in these resolutions of the New York Workingman's party which originally appeared in a pamphlet of December 1829. ☐ John R. Commons, editor, *A Documentary History of American Industrial Society*, Vol. 5, pp. 160, 161, 162–163, 164. Cleveland: The Arthur H. Clark Company, copyright © 1910.

Resolved, that we explicitly disavow all intentions to intermeddle with the rights of individuals, either as to property or religion; but that we hold those rights as sacred as life, not to be approached by ruthless despots or visionary fanatics.

Resolved, that it is wholly incompatible with human rights, that any free citizen, who has duly surrendered all his property to his creditors, should for one moment be deprived of his liberty.

Resolved, that we are in favor of searching laws, for the detection of concealed or fraudulently conveyed property, and emphatically in favor of the entire abolishment of imprisonment for debt. . . .

Resolved, that it is the earnest wish of this meeting, that our representatives in the next legislature, early in the session, introduce and support a bill for the abolishment of imprisonment for debt, and, at all events, that they do not tamely submit to any curtailment of our present jail limits.

Resolved, that, next to life and liberty, we consider education the greatest blessing bestowed upon mankind.

Resolved, that the public funds should be appropriated (to a reasonable extent) to the purposes of education, upon a regular system, that shall ensure the opportunity to every individual of obtaining a competent education before he shall have arrived at the age of maturity.

Resolved, that our sentiments, in relation to a well constructed lien law, which would secure to thousands of our fellow-citizens that just recompense their services entitle them to, and prevent innumerable frauds being practised on the producing classes, are well known to our representatives, and that we expect their efficient support of this measure.

Resolved, that our present militia system is highly oppressive to the producing classes of the community, without any beneficial result to individuals or the state. . . .

Resolved, that the banks, under the administration of their present directors and officers, and by the concert of auctioneers and foreigners, aided by custom house credits, form a monopoly that is hostile to the equal rights of the American merchant, manufacturer, mechanic, and laboring man; and that the renewal, by the legislature, of the charters prayed for, will confirm and perpetuate an aristocracy, which eventually, may shake the foundations of our liberties, and entail slavery on our posterity. . . .

Resolved, that our courts of justice should be so reformed, that the producing classes may be placed on an equality with the wealthy.

Resolved, that the present laws, that compel the attendance of jurors and witnesses, for days and weeks, at our courts, without a fair compensation are unjust and require immediate alteration.

Resolved, that, by affixing enormous bonds to most of the appointed, and many elective offices, our rulers have placed them mostly in the hands of the wealthy or designing politicians and corrupt apostates.

Resolved, that it is our deliberate opinion, that the road to appointed offices has in a great measure been closed against those qualifications which in our estimation should be the only criterion, such as talent, application, and moral virtue. . . .

Resolved, that there should be no intermediate body of men between the electors and the candidates; that the electors have an undoubted right to enjoy a free and open choice of their representatives. . . .

Resolved, that, as faithful sentinels we will guard the temple of our liberties against all further encroachments; that united we will keep the field, and maintain the war, until the justice of our demands shall be fully disseminated and felt throughout the United States, the lost ground regained, and our principles established upon an unchangeable basis.

II

THE DEMAND OF LABOR FOR FREE PUBLIC SCHOOLS

The following selection was taken from a detailed defense of labor's demand for free public schools originally published in the *Working Man's Advocate* of New York City in 1830. Although referring to educational needs in Pennsylvania, the criticisms would have been generally valid against the policies of any state. □ *A Documentary History of American Industrial Society*, Vol. 5, pp. 94, 95–97, 99.

Report of the Joint Committees of the City and County of Philadelphia, appointed September, 1829, to ascertain the state of public instruction in Pennsylvania, and to digest and propose such improvements in education as may be deemed essential to the intellectual and moral prosperity of the people. . . .

The elementary schools throughout the state are irresponsible institutions, established by individuals, from mere motives of private speculation or gain, who are sometimes destitute of character, and frequently, of the requisite attainments and abilities. From the circumstance of the schools being the absolute property of individuals, no supervision or effectual control can be exercised over them; hence, ignorance, inattention, and even immorality, prevail to a lamentable extent among their teachers.

In some districts, no schools whatever exist! No means whatever of acquiring education are resorted to; while ignorance, and its never failing consequence, crime, are found to prevail in these neglected spots, to a greater extent than in other more favored portions of the state. . . .

. . . [The] principles on which . . . "school districts" are founded, are yet . . . extremely defective and inefficient. Their leading feature is pauperism! They are confined exclusively to the children of the poor, while there are, perhaps, thousands of children whose parents are unable to afford for them, a good private education, yet whose standing, professions or connexions in society effectually exclude them from taking the benefit of a poor law. There are great numbers, even of the poorest parents, who hold a dependence on the public bounty to be incompatible with the rights and liberties of an American citizen, and whose deep and cherished consciousness of independence determines them rather to starve the intellect of their offspring, than submit to become the objects of public charity.

There are, also, many poor families, who are totally unable to maintain and clothe their children, while at the schools; and who are compelled to place them, at a very early age, at some kind of labor that may assist in supporting them, or to bind them out as apprentices to relieve themselves entirely of the burthen of their maintenance and education. . . .

Another radical and glaring defect in the existing public school system is the very limited amount of instruction it affords, even to the comparatively small number of youth, who enjoy its benefits. It extends, in no case, further than a tolerable proficiency in reading, writing, and arithmetic, and sometimes to a slight acquaintance with geography. Besides these, the girls are taught a few simple branches of industry. A great proportion of scholars, however, from the causes already enumerated, acquire but a very slight and partial knowledge of these branches. . . .

The original element of despotism is a monopoly of talent, which consigns the multitude to comparative ignorance, and secures the balance of knowledge on the side of the rich and the rulers. If then the healthy existence of a free government be, as the committee believe, rooted in the will of the American people, it follows as a necessary consequence, of a government based upon that will, that this monopoly should be broken up, and that the means of equal knowledge, (the only security for equal liberty) should be rendered, by legal provision, the common property of all classes.

In a republic, the people constitute the government, and by wielding its powers in accordance with the dictates, either of their intelligence or their ignorance; of their judgment or their caprices, are the makers and the rulers of their own good or evil destiny. They frame the laws and create the institutions, that promote their happiness or produce their destruction. If they be wise and intelligent, no laws but what are just and equal will receive their approbation, or be sustained by their suffrages. If they be ignorant and capricious, they will be deceived by mistaken or designing rulers, into the support of laws that are unequal and unjust.

III

A CRITIC OF FREE PUBLIC EDUCATION

Although not written in reply to the article in the *Working Man's Advocate,* the following excerpt from an editorial of March 6, 1830, appearing in the Philadelphia *National Gazette,* summarizes the arguments of the opponents of free public education. ⊔ *A Documentary History of American Industrial Society,* Vol. 5, pp. 110–112.

We can readily pardon the editor of the United States *Gazette* for not perceiving that the scheme of Universal Equal Education at the expense of the State, is virtually "Agrarianism." It would be a compulsory application of the means of the richer, for the direct use of the poorer classes; and so far an arbitrary division of property among them. The declared object is, to procure the opportunity of instruction for the child or children of every citizen; to elevate the standard of the education of the working classes, or equalize the standard for all classes; which would, doubtless, be to lower or narrow that which the rich may now compass. But the most sensible and reflecting possessors of property sufficient to enable them to educate their children in the most liberal and efficacious way, and upon the broadest scale, would prefer to share their means for any other purpose, or in any other mode, than such as would injuriously affect or circumscribe the proficiency of their offspring. A public meeting of "the Mechanics and other Working Men of the City and County of New York," was held in the city, on the 17th inst., and among the principles for which they have "resolved" to contend, we find the following:

"In Education—The adoption of a general system of instruction, at the expense of the State, which shall afford to children, however rich or poor, equal means to obtain useful learning. To effect this, it is believed that a system of direct taxation will not be necessary, as the surplus revenue of the State and United States Governments will, in a very few years, afford ample means—but even if it were necessary to resort to direct taxation to accomplish this all-important object, and the amount paid by the wealthy should be far greater than that paid by our less eligibly situated fellow-citizens, an equivalent to them would be found in the increased ability and usefulness of the educated citizen to serve and to promote the best interests of the State; in the increased permanency of our institutions—and in the superior protection of liberty, person and property."

Thus, a direct tax for "the equal means of obtaining useful learning" is not deemed improbable, and it is admitted that the amount which would be paid by the wealthy would be "far greater" than that paid by their "less eligibly situated fellow citizens." Here, we contend, would be the action, if not the name, of the Agrarian system. Authority—that is, the State—is to force the more eligibly situated citizens to contribute a part (which might be very considerable) of their means, for the accommodation of the rest; and this is equivalent to the idea of an actual, compulsory partition of their substance. The more thriving members of the "mechanical and other working classes" would themselves feel the evil of the direct taxation; they would find that they had toiled for the benefit of other families than their own. One of the chief excitements to industry, among those classes, is the hope of earning the means of educating their children respectably or liberally: that incentive would be removed, and the scheme of State and equal education be thus a premium for comparative idleness, to be taken out of the pockets of the laborious and conscientious. . . .

We have no confidence in any compulsory equalizations; it has been well observed that they pull down what is above, but never much raise what is below, and often "depress high and low together beneath the level of what was originally the lowest." By no possibility could a perfect equality be procured. A scheme of universal equal education, attempted in reality, would be an unexampled bed of Procrustes, for the understandings of our youth, and in fact, could not be used with any degree of equality of profit, unless the dispositions and circumstances of parents and children were nearly the same; to accomplish which phenomenon, in a nation of many millions, engaged in a great variety of pursuits, would be beyond human power.

IV

DEMANDING THE TEN-HOUR DAY

This reading was taken from a circular that was issued to support a strike of the building trades in Boston in 1835. The strike failed, but the circular furnished an incentive to workers in other cities to follow Boston's example. In many cases, these subsequent strikes succeeded. ☐ John R. Commons, editor, *A Documentary History of American Industrial Society,* Vol. 6, pp. 94–95, 96–99. New York: Russell & Russell, Inc., copyright © 1958.

At a very large and respectable Meeting of House Carpenters, Masons and Stone Cutters, assembled in Julien Hall, Boston, May 4, 1835, to consider the subject of the hours of labor in order that Ten Hours should at all times constitute a day's work, the Undersigned were appointed a Committee to address a Circular to our brethren in all branches of Mechanical labor in the City, the Commonwealth and elsewhere, to inform them of the state of things in this City, relative to the subject under consideration. . . .

The work in which we are now engaged is neither more nor less than a contest between Money and Labor: Capital, which can only be made productive by labor, is endeavoring to crush labor the only source of all wealth.

We have been too long subjected to the odious, cruel, unjust, and tyrannical system which compels the operative Mechanic to exhaust his physical and mental powers by excessive toil, until he has no desire but to eat and sleep, and in many cases he has no power to do either from extreme debility.

We contend that no man or body of men, have a right to require of us that we should toil as we have hitherto done under the old system of labor.

We go further. No man or body of men who require such excessive labor can be friends to the country or the Rights of Man. We also say, that we have rights, and we have duties to perform as American Citizens and members of society, which forbid us to dispose of more than Ten Hours for a day's work.

We cannot, we will not, longer be mere slaves to inhuman, insatiable and unpitying avarice. We have taken a firm and decided stand, to obtain the acknowledgment of those rights to enable us to perform those duties to God, our Country and ourselves. . . .

. . . Our opposers resort to the most degrading obloquy to injure us. Not degrading to us, but to the authors of such unmerited opprobrium which they attempt to cast upon us. They tell us "We shall spend all our hours of leisure in Drunkenness and Debauchery if the hours of labor are reduced."

We assert and challenge the world to controvert the position that excessive labor has been the immediate cause of more intemperance than all other causes combined. Physical exhaustion craves and will have excitement of some kind, and the cause of Temperance never will prevail until slavery among Mechanics shall cease from the land.

We are friends to temperance "in all things," but any man who requires of us excessive labor is intemperate; if he is not actuated by ardent spirits, he is controlled by a spirit of inhumanity equally fatal to human happiness. . . .

To show the utter fallacy of their idiotic reasoning, if reasoning it may be called, we have only to say, they employ us about eight months in the year during the longest and the hottest days, and in short days, hundreds of us remain idle for want of work, for three or four months, when our expenses must of course be the heaviest during winter. When the long days again appear, our guardians set us to work as they say, "to keep us from getting drunk." No fear has ever been expressed by these benevolent employers respecting our morals while we are idle in short days, through their avarice. We would not be too severe on our employers, they are slaves to the Capitalists, as we are to them. "The power behind" their "throne is greater than the throne itself." But we cannot bear to be the servant of servants and slaves to oppression, let the source be where it may. We will be so no longer, for it is rank injustice. Further, they threaten to starve us into submission to their will. Starve us to prevent us from getting drunk! Wonderful Wisdom! Refined Benevolence! Exalted Philanthropy! . . .

. . . We claim by the blood of our fathers, shed on our battlefields in the War of the Revolution, the rights of American Freemen, and no earthly power shall resist our righteous claims with impunity. . . .

Mechanics of Boston—stand firm—be true to yourselves. Now is the time to enroll your names on the scroll of history as the undaunted enemies of oppression, as the enemies of mental, moral and physical degradation, as the friends of the human race.

The God of the Universe has given us time, health and strength. We utterly deny the right of any man to dictate to us how much of it we shall sell. Brethren in the City, Towns and Country, our cause is yours, the cause of Liberty, the cause of God.

Respectfully yours,

A. H. WOOD, SETH LUTHER, LEVI ABELL
—*Committee.*

Editors of newspapers in the United States who are in favor of equal rights, are respectfully requested to publish this Circular.

Boston, May 8, 1835. THE COMMITTEE

V

THE FIGHT AGAINST THE BANKS

Thomas Skidmore, a prominent reformer during the Jackson era, was responsible for the following resolutions condemning banks and bankers. □ *A Documentary History of American Industrial Society,* Vol. 5, pp. 151–152.

Resolved, that it has become the duty of the people to enquire into the causes of their distresses, and to express their opinions in relation thereto. . . .

Resolved, that these calamities have been greatly aggravated and increased by a legislation which has employed all its energy to create and sustain exclusive privileges; and that among the objects of such privileges, banking institutions stand most conspicuous.

Resolved, that these institutions, as it regards our own state, stand constantly indebted to the public, according to the best of our information, in the sum of thirty or thirty-five millions of dollars.

Resolved, if they are to be suffered to remain among us, that they ought no less to pay interest on the debt they owe to the community, than that the community itself should pay interest on any debt it may owe them.

Resolved, as banking is now conducted, the owners of the banks receive annually, of the people of this state, not less than two millions of dollars, as interest on their paper money, (and it might as well be pewter money,) for which there is and can be nothing provided for its redemption on demand.

Resolved, in this view of the matter, that the greatest knaves, imposters, and paupers of the age, are our bankers; who swear they have promised to pay to their debtors thirty or thirty-five millions of dollars on demand, at the same time that they have, as they also swear, only three, four, or five millions to do it with.

Resolved, that more than one hundred broken banks, within a few years past, admonish the community to destroy banks altogether.

Resolved, that more than a thousand kinds of counterfeit bank notes, from five hundred dollars down to a single dollar, give double force to the admonition.

Resolved, that the Constitution of the United States declares, among other things, that no state shall emit bills of credit; and that, in the opinion of this meeting, all our banking institutions are palpable infractions of that instrument; since if the state, of itself, have not power to emit such bills, it cannot have the power to authorize others to do it.

PROBLEM 5

Rise and Decline of the Knights of Labor

Hard times following the Panic of 1837 brought a decline of local and national unions and turned the organizational efforts of workers in a new direction. During the 1840's, especially, strikes and union activity were all but abandoned, and interest became centered in various reform programs. In many places workers were involved in producers' and consumers' cooperatives of a utopian or visionary character. Some were attracted by cooperative communities designed to reduce unemployment. Others favored a movement to have the national government furnish homesteads to create self-employment for workers.

Trade unions revived again by the beginning of the 1850's. Many national unions were founded, and strikes again became common in almost every large American city. The decade of the 1860's began with a trend toward improved conditions for workers, and the Civil War, with its demands for war goods, furthered the revival of labor organizations.

Local trade unions blossomed, coordinated their activities through city-central labor unions, and erected national unions in some thirty trades. In 1866 representatives of both city and national organizations founded the National Labor Union, the first congress to represent all organized labor since

1837. Three years later nine Philadelphia tailors founded the Noble Order of the Knights of Labor, a secret society devoted vaguely to replacing the "wages system" with the "universal brotherhood of labor."

The depression of 1873–1879 almost destroyed these organizations, but the return of prosperity revitalized them. They advocated reduction of the working day to eight hours, union control of wages, and the formation of cooperative enterprises by workers as an avenue of escape from the insecurities of wage labor. Although the National Labor Union ceased to function after 1872, both the idea of a national congress of trade unions and the broad reform platform it had espoused gained new life. The reform platform of the N.L.U. was inherited by the Knights of Labor.

Under the leadership of Terence V. Powderly, a scholarly machinist who became "Grand Master Workman" of the Order in 1879, the Knights became the main center of labor activity in the nation. Open to workers regardless of occupation, race, nationality, or sex, and excluding bankers, lawyers, gamblers, and liquor dealers, the Order grew to more than 700,000 members by 1886. This growth created dilemmas which ultimately were the undoing of the Knights. Powderly abhorred strikes and sought the arbitration of all industrial disputes. Arbitration was often impossible, however, because employers refused to meet with or recognize bargaining agents selected by the workingmen. Time and again, therefore, the Knights conducted massive strikes. These strikes in turn produced local leaders who spurned Powderly's conciliatory policies.

The strains within the Order were brought to a head when the Federation of Organized Trades and Labor Unions of North America called for nationwide strikes on May 1, 1886. This organization, which was a forerunner of the American Federation of Labor, was out to win the eight-hour day. Powderly was unable to restrain his followers from joining the call, and strikes swept the land. In Chicago, where anarchists placed themselves at the head of the movement, a bomb was hurled at police in Haymarket Square. This incident unleashed a wave of violent repression against the labor movement. While press and police associated all labor organizations with violence, many workers charged Powderly with timidity. The Knights cracked under the strain and declined rapidly.

The readings which follow attempt to trace important developments in the history of the American labor movement during the period when the Knights of Labor rose to prominence and then gave way to new leadership. Keep the following questions in mind as you read:

1   Does the Statement of Principles reveal the specific goals of the Knights? How could union members reach the goals listed in this statement?

2   What seems to be behind Powderly's opposition to the strike as a weapon of organized labor? What alternative action does he propose? Is he realistic? Explain.

3   How do you account for the tone of the language used in the Revenge Circular? Would attitudes like the ones revealed here have been as likely to develop if capitalists had bargained collectively with chosen representatives of their workers?

4   What issues lay behind the split in the leadership of the Knights? What dangers were inherent in this division?

5   Why were many Americans willing to believe that the Knights advocated anarchy and violence?

6   Was the philosophy of Powderly practical? How could he have won benefits for his followers without the strike? What does your conclusion contribute to an understanding of the issue of why the Knights failed?

I

A STATEMENT OF PRINCIPLES

The following excerpt includes the preamble and the first two points in the platform of the Knights of Labor. It is taken from a circular issued to the public in 1882. □ *Annual Report of the Secretary of Internal Affairs of the Commonwealth of Pennsylvania, Part 3, Industrial Statistics,* Vol. 15, p. G. 33. Harrisburg: E. K. Meyers, 1888.

The alarming development and aggression of aggregated wealth, which, unless checked, will inevitably lead to the pauperization and hopeless . . . [degradation] of the toiling masses, renders it imperative, if we desire to enjoy the blessings of life, that a check should be placed upon its power and upon unjust accumulation, and a system adopted which will secure to the laborer the fruits of his toil; and as this much desired object can only be accomplished by the thorough unification of those who labor, and the united efforts of those who earn their bread by the sweat of their brow, we have formed the order of the KNIGHTS OF LABOR, with a view of securing the organization and direction, by coöperative effort of the power of the industrial classes; and we submit to the world the objects sought to be accomplished by our organization, calling upon all who believe in securing "the greatest good to the greatest number" to aid and assist us.

I. To bring within the folds of organization every department of productive industry, making knowledge a standpoint for action, and industrial, moral worth, not wealth, the true standard of individual and national greatness.

II. To secure to the toilers a proper share of the wealth that they create; more of the leisure that rightfully belongs to them; more society advantages; more of the benefits, privileges and emoluments of the world; in a word, all those rights and privileges necessary to make them capable of enjoying, appreciating, defending and perpetuating the blessings of good government.

II

POWDERLY ON USE OF THE STRIKE

In this excerpt from his autobiography, Grand Master Workman Powderly reveals his attitude toward strikes. ☐ Terence V. Powderly, *The Path I Trod*, pp. 104–105. New York: Columbia University Press, copyright © 1940.

It never was the intention of those who founded and built up the Knights of Labor to resort to the strike as first aid in the settlement of differences between employer and employed. Don't forget that the founders were all trade unionists who had seen the futility of ill-advised, hastily begun strikes.

Here let me say that I don't know, and never knew, an officer of a labor organization who favors or favored the strike except as a last effort to effect a redress of grievances. The public has been educated to believe that labor leaders, as they are called, just glory in and fatten on strikes. Prior to my first election as Grand Master Workman I . . . stated that I would never favor a strike until I became convinced:

First: That the cause was just

Second: That every reasonable means had been resorted to to avert the strike

Third: That the chances of winning were at least as good as the prospect of losing

Fourth: That the means of defraying the expenses of the strike and assisting those in need were in the treasury or in sight of it. . . .

Where a strike was forced on us, as it frequently was, the case would differ from one in which we, as an organization, declared a strike. We would have to defend ourselves as best we could. In no such case did I ever fail, or refuse, to do every legitimate thing in my power to win a strike so forced on us. Not once did I, during my fourteen years' incumbency of the office of General Master Workman, order a strike.

III

THE MILITANT VIEW

Not all local leaders of the Knights of Labor agreed with Powderly on labor methods. The following excerpt is from the famous "Revenge Circular" issued in 1886 by Martin Irons, a western leader of the Knights, during the strike against the Southwest Railroad System controlled by the financier Jay Gould. □ House Document No. 4174, 49th Congress, 2nd Session, 1886–1887, Part 1, pp. 41, 42.

TO THE WORKINGMEN OF THE WORLD: . . .

Gould the giant fiend, Gould the money monarch, is dancing, as he claims, over the grave of our order, over the ruin of our homes and the blight of our lives. . . .

Brother workmen, this monster fiend has compelled many of us to toil in cold and rain for 5 and 50 cents a day. Others have been compelled to yield their time to him for seventeen and thirty-six weary hours for the pittance of nine hours' pay. Others who have dared to assert their manhood and rebel against this tyranny are black-listed and boycotted all over the land. . . .

He lives under and enjoys all the benefits of a republican form of government and yet advocates and perpetuates the most debasing form of white slavery. He robs the rich and poor, the high and low, with ruthless hand, and then appeals to corrupt and purchased courts to help him take our little homes away. He breaks our limbs and maims our bodies and then demands that we shall release him from every claim for damage or be black-listed forever.

He goes to our grocers and persuades them not to give us credit because we refuse to be ground in his human mill. He turns upon us a horde of lawless thugs, who shoot among our wives and children with deadly intent, and then he howls for Government help when he gets his pay in coin alike.

Fellow workmen, Gould must be overthrown. His giant power must be broken, or you and I must be slaves forever. The Knights of Labor alone have dared to be a David to this Goliath. The battle is not for to-day—the battle is not for to-morrow—but for the trooping generations in the coming ages of the world, for our children and our children's children. 'Tis the great question of the age—shall we, in the coming ages, be a nation of freemen or a nation of slaves? . . .

Workmen of the world, marshal yourselves upon the battle-field. Workmen of every trade and clime, into the fray! Gould and his monopolies must go down, or your children must be slaves.

IV

DIVIDED LEADERSHIP

The following selection, taken from an editorial in the Fort Worth *Gazette*, discusses the split in leadership of the Knights of Labor. The item is appropriately titled. □ "A House Divided Against Itself," Fort Worth, Texas: *The Gazette,* April 11, 1886, p. 4.

That there are two factions inside the order is incontestable. Each wants to rule. Neither is satisfied with the rule of the other. Mr. Powderly may be accepted as the representative of one class, and Martin Irons of the other. Powderly is a conservative; Irons a fanatic. Powderly would bring industrial and social relief by working upon and obliterating the causes of social and industrial ills, Irons would cure the disease by killing the patient. Powderly is a philosopher, Irons is a socialist. Each has a following among the members of the organization. The men who are for peace stand by Powderly. The incendiaries, anarchists and the ignorant element sustain Irons. One of two things must happen: the Powderly or Irons faction must triumph and the other submit; or the organization must split, and each faction cling to its leader.

. . . The highly intelligent central executive board, with Mr. Powderly as its chief, does not control the action of the subordinate assemblies . . . . The present strike not only was not ordered by the chief of the order, without whose approval no general action should ever be taken, but it has come under his condemnation as unnecessary and premature. . . .

Irons says that Powderly has no authority to command him what he shall or shall not do. If he has not, then there is virtually no organization, for there is no head. If Powderly has the right to direct Irons, and he refuses to obey orders, then comes mutiny, and if the chief is not sustained and the recalcitrant subordinate [not] punished, there is no discipline and no organization. If Powderly should attempt to coerce Irons, it is very plain that a schism will ensue, for in this part of the country the members look more to Irons than to Powderly for direction.

The more sensible and far-seeing among the Knights themselves foresee and tremble at this danger. Probably, however, it would be no real loss . . . if . . . the more violent secede . . . and set up [an organization] for themselves. . . . The seceders would very quickly get to fighting among themselves, and break up. If the split is to come, Mr. Powderly could not welcome a better time than the present. He should take the bull by the horns and insist that Irons shall obey him or get out and let whoever will follow him.

V

DISSENSION IN THE RANKS

Many rank and file members of the Knights of Labor favored use of the strike and agreed with a proposal calling for work stoppage on May 1, 1886. Anticipating this possibility, Powderly issued a secret circular against the eight-hour movement to local assemblies of the Order. □ Terence V. Powderly, *Thirty Years of Labor, 1859–1889,* p. 496. Columbus, Ohio: Excelsior Publishing House, 1890.

No assembly of the Knights of Labor must strike for the eight hour system on May first under the impression that they are obeying orders from headquarters, for such an order was not, and will not, be given. Neither employer or employe are educated to the needs and necessities for the short hour plan. If one branch of trade or one assembly is in such a condition, remember that there are many who are in total ignorance of the movement. Out of the sixty millions of people in the United States and Canada, our order has possibly three hundred thousand. Can we mould the sentiment of the millions in favor of the short hour plan before May first? It is nonsense to think of it. Let us learn why our hours of labor should be reduced, and then teach others.

VI

THE EXTREMIST VIEW

The ranks of labor included groups which would go beyond the process of peaceful striking. The next reading is from the platform of an anarchist group, The International Working People's Association. It was published in the *Alarm,* a Chicago newspaper edited by Albert Parsons, who was one of those later executed as a result of the Haymarket bombing. □ Joseph E. Gary, "The Chicago Anarchists of 1886: The Crime, the Trial, and the Punishment," *The Century Magazine,* Vol. 45, No. 6, April, 1893, p. 813.

The present order of society is based upon the spoliation of the non-property by the property owners, the capitalists buy the labor of the poor for wages, at the mere cost of living, taking all the surplus of labor. . . . Thus while the poor are increasingly deprived the opportunities of advancement, the rich grow richer through increasing robbery. . . . The system is unjust, insane, and murderous. Therefore those who suffer under it, and do not wish to be responsible for its continuance, ought to strive for its destruction by all means and with their utmost energy. . . . The laborers can look for aid from no outside source in their fight against the existing system, but must achieve deliverance through their own exertions. Hitherto, no privileged class have relinquished tyranny, nor will the capitalists of today forego their privilege and authority without compulsion. . . . It is therefore self-evident that the fight of proletarianism against the bourgeoisie must have a violent revolutionary character; that wage conflicts cannot lead to the goal. . . . Under all these circumstances, there is only one remedy left—force. . . . Agitation to organize, organizations for the purpose of rebellion, this is the course if the workingmen would rid themselves of their chains.

VII

CALL TO ACTION: THE HAYMARKET AFFAIR

Strikers at the McCormick Harvester works in Chicago were fired upon by policemen on May 3, 1886, and several were killed. Soon afterward the following appeal was written and circularized by August Spies, an anarchist. He also was among those executed as a result of the riot in Haymarket Square. □ M. J. Schaack, *Anarchy and Anarchists: A History of the Red Terror and the Social Revolution in America and Europe*, p. 130. Chicago: F. J. Schulte & Company, 1889.

REVENGE!

WORKINGMEN, TO ARMS!!!

Your masters sent out their bloodhounds—the police—; they killed six of your brothers at McCormicks this afternoon. They killed the poor wretches because they, like you, had the courage to disobey the supreme will of your bosses. They killed them because they dared ask for the shortening of the hours of toil. They killed them to show you, "Free American Citizens" that you must be satisfied and . . . [contented] with whatever your bosses condescend to allow you, or you will get killed!

You have for years endured the most abject humiliations; you have for years suffered unmeasurable iniquities; you have worked yourself to death; you have endured the pangs of want and hunger; your Children you have sacrificed to the factory-lords—in short: You have been miserable and obedient . . . [slaves] all these years: Why? To satisfy the insatiable greed, to fill the coffers of your lazy thieving master? When you ask them now to lessen your burden, he sends his bloodhounds out to shoot you, kill you!

If you are men, if you are the sons of your grand sires, who have shed their blood to free you, then you will rise in your might, Hercules, and destroy the hideous monster that seeks to destroy you. To arms we call you, to arms!

YOUR BROTHERS

This reproduction of a handbill printed in English and in German announces a meeting to protest the shooting of striking McCormick workers. At this meeting the famous riot occurred in which a bomb was thrown into the ranks of the police. Seven policemen were fatally injured and scores were wounded. Eight anarchist leaders were rounded up and charged with the murders. □ An Anarchist Handbill, *The Century Magazine*, Vol. 45, No. 6, April 1893, p. 826.

VIII

REPUDIATION OF ANARCHISTS BY THE KNIGHTS

Although many labor leaders rallied to the defense of the accused anarchists, Powderly and the leaders of the Knights quickly and publicly dissociated themselves from the events in Chicago by the following editorial. ☐ Chicago: *Knights of Labor,* Vol. 1, No. 5, May 8, 1886.

Let it be understood by all the world that the Knights of Labor have no affiliation, association, sympathy or respect for the band of cowardly murderers, cutthroats and robbers, known as anarchists, who sneak through the country, like midnight assassins, stirring up the passions of ignorant foreigners, unfurling the red flag of anarchy and causing riot and bloodshed. Parsons, Spies, Fielding, Most and all their followers, sympathizers, aiders and abettors should be summarily dealt with. They are entitled to no more consideration than wild beasts. The leaders are cowards and their followers are fools.

Knights of Labor, boycott them; if one of the gang of scoundrels should by any mistake get access to our organization expel them at once, brand them as outlawed monsters . . . as human monstrosities not entitled to the sympathy or consideration of any person in the world.

IX

JUSTICE OR HYSTERIA?

In the trial of the eight anarchists which followed, it was never proven who actually threw the bomb. On strictly circumstantial evidence all were found guilty and sentenced to be executed. Four of them were hanged, one committed suicide in jail, and three were subsequently pardoned by Governor John P. Altgeld of Illinois. The following excerpt from Governor Altgeld's pardon message gives his views of the atmosphere in which the trial of the anarchists was held. ☐ John P. Altgeld, *The Chicago Martyrs,* p. 153. San Francisco: Free Society Publishers, 1899.

It is further shown here that much of the evidence given at the trial was a pure fabrication; that some of the prominent police officials, in their zeal, not only terrorized ignorant men by throwing them into prison and threatening them with torture if they refused to swear to anything desired, but that they offered money and employment to those who would consent to do this. Further, that they deliberately planned to have fictitious conspiracies formed in order that they might get the glory of discovering them. In addition to the evidence in the record of some witnesses who swore that they had been paid small sums of money, etc., several documents are here referred to.

X

WHY THE KNIGHTS FAILED

Powderly himself sums up the problems which contributed to the decline of the Knights of Labor in the following letter written in 1893. □ Norman J. Ware, *The Labor Movement in the United States*, pp. 375–376. New York: D. Appleton & Company, copyright © 1929.

Teacher of important and much-needed reforms [the Knights of Labor], she has been obliged to practice differently from her teachings. Advocating arbitration and conciliation as first steps in labor disputes she has been forced to take upon her shoulders the responsibilities of the aggressor first and, when hope of arbitrating and conciliation failed, to beg of the opposing side to do what we should have applied for in the first instance. Advising against strikes we have been in the midst of them. Urging important reforms we have been forced to yield our time and attention to petty disputes until we were placed in a position where we have frequently been misunderstood by the employee as well as the employer. While not a political party we have been forced into the attitude of taking political action. . . . All these things have had their effect in reducing our membership but through all the turmoil and misunderstanding the Order has stamped deep its impression for good upon the records of the world and should it collapse to-night those who survive it may point to its splendid achievements in forcing to the front the cause of misunderstood and down-trodden humanity.

PROBLEM 6

Organizing the
American Federation of Labor

The growth of national trade unions of skilled craftsmen paralleled the rise of the Knights of Labor. The idea that each trade should have a highly centralized and well-financed union was fostered by new and aggressive labor leadership, represented by such men as Samuel Gompers of the Cigar-Makers' Union and Peter J. McGuire of the Carpenters' Union.

Far narrower in their objectives and more exclusive in their membership, the national trade unions found themselves increasingly in conflict with the Knights. In many places both a trade union and a local assembly of Knights competed for recognition as sole bargaining agent of the same group of workers. An attempt to settle differences between the rivals occurred in May 1886 at a conference of the leaders of twenty national unions held in Philadelphia. A "treaty" was drafted and presented to the Knights in an attempt to eliminate competition between the two groups. The Knights, whose membership at the time was easily five times the combined size of the national trade unions, rejected the proposal.

In response to this refusal, the trade unionists issued a call for a convention to be held in Columbus, Ohio, in December 1886. At this convention the American Federation of Labor was created. The use of the word *federa-*

tion in the title of the new organization reflected one of its cardinal principles. Each union was to be autonomous, or independent, in its trade, but all unions were united for mutual assistance. Samuel Gompers was elected president, and Peter J. McGuire became secretary. The trade-union ideals of these two men profoundly influenced the new federation. While the Knights of Labor languished, craft unions thrived in the same national atmosphere.

The national unions in the American Federation of Labor were organized among workers whose skill or strategic position in an industry gave them bargaining power with their employers. The unions in the building trades provide classic examples. With few exceptions, their members were highly skilled and could not be replaced by strikebreakers who had not been trained. If one building-trades union, such as the plasterers, struck, the members of the other unions would not cross the picket lines. Since builders often had huge sums of money tied up in a project, they were anxious to have contractors settle with a union so that the building could be completed and become a source of income. Hence, a strike in the building industry could often bring employers quickly to their knees.

Gompers and his colleagues knew these economic facts of life. They believed that if both skilled and unskilled workers were enrolled in the same union, the unskilled men with little bargaining power would soon exhaust the union treasury in strikes which they had little chance to win. So they built a federation of the skilled men who could hope for success. Not until the New Deal of Franklin D. Roosevelt changed the bargaining situation in the 1930's could unskilled workers join the ranks of organized labor in significant numbers.

The readings in Problem 6 attempt to show how the American Federation of Labor gained prominence as the leading organization representing skilled workers in the United States.

Think of the following questions as you read:

1   In what ways did the cigar-making trade offer excellent leadership preparation for Samuel Gompers?

2   What basic objections to the Knights of Labor are voiced by Gompers in Reading II? Are they justified?

3   Which provisions of the "treaty" in Reading III might have been most objectionable to the Knights of Labor?

4   Do you agree with the logic in Gompers' argument that strong unions tend to prevent boycotts and strikes and thus are desirable? Explain.

5   Do you agree with Gompers that labor should be nonpartisan in politics? How do you think this position would affect the bargaining power of labor?

I

LIFE OF THE CIGAR-MAKER

In his autobiography, Samuel Gompers, one of the founders of the American Federation of Labor, described working conditions and union practices in the cigar-making industry during the period following the Civil War. □ From the book *Seventy Years of Life and Labor* by Samuel Gompers, pp. 43, 44, 45. Copyright ©, 1925, by E. P. Dutton & Co., Inc. Renewal, 1952, by Gertrude Cleaves Gompers. Reprinted by permission of the publishers.

There was a vast difference between those early unions and the unions of today. Then there was no law or order. A union was a more or less definite group of people employed in the same trade who might help each other out in special difficulties with the employer. There was no sustained effort to secure fair wages through collective bargaining. The employer fixed wages until he shoved them down to a point where human endurance revolted. Often the revolt started by an individual whose personal grievance was sore, who rose and declared: "I am going on strike. All who remain at work are scabs." Usually the workers went out with him.

I remember being busily at work one day when Conrad Kuhn, president of the Cigarmakers' Unions of New York City, entered the shop and announced: "This shop is on strike." Kuhn was a large, fine-looking man, with a stentorian voice that could be heard in every portion of the shop. Without hesitation we all laid down our work and walked out. That was the way it was done in the early days. We had no conception of constructive business tactics beginning with presentation of demands and negotiation to reach an agreement.

Whether we won or lost that strike I don't remember, but the union had no money at the end. . . .

The union was generally in a precarious condition financially. Strike funds were never assured, and there were no other benefits. The union represented a feeling of community of burdens of those working in the same industry. It had to acquire a new meaning before it became an industrial agency. It had to strengthen its defensive resources and develop cohesive forces. But that was not only the embryonic stage of unionism; it was the fledgling period of industry. Industrial production was uncouth, unscientific, just about as planless as unionism. Management, accountancy, salesmanship, elimination of waste were in the rule-of-thumb stage. Factory architecture and industrial sanitation were undeveloped sciences.

Any kind of an old loft served as a cigar shop. If there were enough windows, we had sufficient light for our work; if not, it was apparently no concern of the management. There was an entirely different conception of sanitation both in the shop and in the home of those days from now. The toilet facilities were a water-closet and a sink for washing purposes, usually located by the closet. In most cigar shops our towels were the bagging that came around the bales of Havana and other high grades of tobacco. . . .

The tobacco leaf was prepared by strippers who drew the leaves from the heavy stem and put them in pads of about fifty. The leaves had to be handled carefully to prevent tearing. The craftsmanship of the cigarmaker was shown in his ability to utilize wrappers to the best advantage to shave off the unusable to a hairbreadth, to roll so as to cover holes in the leaf and to use both hands so as to make a perfectly shaped and rolled product. These things a good cigarmaker learned to do more or less mechanically, which left us free to think, talk, listen, or sing. I loved the freedom of that work, for I had earned the mind-freedom that accompanied skill as a craftsman. I was eager to learn from discussion and reading or to pour out my feeling in song. Often we chose someone to read to us who was a particularly good reader, and in payment the rest of us gave him sufficient of our cigars so he was not the loser. The reading was always followed by discussion, so we learned to know each other pretty thoroughly. We learned who could take a joke in good spirit, who could marshal his thoughts in an orderly way, who could distinguish clever sophistry from sound reasoning. The fellowship that grew between congenial shopmates was something that lasted a lifetime.

II

COMPARING THE KNIGHTS AND TRADE UNIONISM

In the selection below, Gompers compares the goals of the Knights with aims of trade unionists, indicating why the latter broke away to form their own organization. □ From the book *Seventy Years of Life and Labor* by Samuel Gompers, pp. 244–245, 274. Copyright ©, 1925, by E. P. Dutton & Co., Inc. Renewal, 1952, by Gertrude Cleaves Gompers. Reprinted by permission of the publishers.

After my initiation into the K. of L. in the 'seventies, I heard of it now and then but never as a substitute for trade unions. With the 'eighties, when it abandoned complete secrecy, it grew much more rapidly. . . .

. . . Trade unions endeavored to organize for collective responsibility persons with common trade problems. They sought economic betterment in order to place in the hands of wage-earners the means to wider opportunities. The Knights of Labor was a social or fraternal organization. It was based upon a principle of co-operation and its purpose was reform. The K. of L. prided itself upon being something higher and grander than a trade union or political party. Unfortunately, its purposes were not always exemplified through the declarations and the acts of its members. The order admitted to membership any person, excluding only lawyers and saloon-keepers. This policy included employers among those eligible. Larger employers gradually withdrew from the order, but the small employers and small business men and politicians remained. The order was a hodge-podge with no basis for solidarity with the exception of a comparatively few trade assemblies. . . .

When the order began to encroach upon the economic field, trouble was inevitable, for such invasion was equivalent to setting up a dual organization to perform a task for which they were entirely unfitted. It was particularly unfortunate when it endeavored to conduct strikes. The K. of L. was a highly centralized organization and this often placed decision upon essential trade policies in the hands of officers outside the trade concerned. Strikes are essentially an expression of collective purpose of workers who perform related services and who have the spirit of union growing out of joint employment. The K. of L. never engaged in any dispute with employers, large or small, but that they received the support of trade unionists including myself. . . .

The struggle between trade unions and the K. of L. was at high tide when I assumed the task of making the American Federation of Labor something more than a paper organization.

III

A PEACE OFFERING

The following reading is the "treaty" drafted and presented to the Knights of Labor by the Philadelphia trade-union conference of May 1886. ⊔ *Record of the Proceedings,* Special Session, General Assembly of the Knights of Labor, May-June 1886, Cleveland, p. 12.

1st. That in any branch of labor having a National or International Trade Union, the Knights of Labor shall not initiate any person or form any Assembly of persons following a trade or calling organized under such National or International Union without the consent of the nearest Local Union of the National or International Union affected.

2[d.] No person shall be admitted to membership in the Knights of Labor who works for less than the regular scale of wages fixed by the trade union of his craft or calling, and none shall be admitted to membership in the Knights of Labor who have ever been convicted of "scabbing," "ratting," embezzlement or any other offense against the union of his trade or calling until exonerated by said union.

3[d.] That the charter of any Knights of Labor Assembly of any trade having a National or International Union shall be revoked, and the members of the same be requested to join a mixed Assembly or form a local Union under the jurisdiction of their National or International Trade Union.

4[th.] That any Organizer of the Knights of Labor who endeavors to induce trade unions to disband or tampers with their growth or privileges, shall have his commission forthwith revoked.

5[th.] That wherever a strike of any trade union is in progress no Assembly or District Assembly of the Knights of Labor shall interfere until settled to the satisfaction of the trade union affected.

6[th.] That the Knights of Labor shall not establish or issue any trade mark or label in competition with any trade mark or label now issued, or that may be hereafter issued by any National or International Trade Union.

IV

CREATING THE A. F. OF L.

Soon after the General Assembly of the Knights rejected the "treaty," a conference of trade-union leaders was called at which the American Federation of Labor was born. The excerpt below is part of the call explaining the structure and aims of the new federation. □ Morton A. Aldrich, "The American Federation of Labor," *Economic Studies*, Vol. 3, No. 4, August 1898, p. 232. New York: The Macmillan Company. Copyright © 1898 by the American Economic Association.

The objects of the American Federation of Labor are stated in its constitution as follows:

1. The objects of this Federation shall be the encouragement and formation of local Trade and Labor Unions, and the closer federation of such societies through the organization of Central Trade and Labor Unions in every city, and the further combination of such bodies, into State, Terri-

torial, or Provincial organizations, to secure legislation in the interest of the working masses.

2. The establishment of National and International Trade Unions, based upon a strict recognition of the autonomy of each trade, and the promotion and advancement of such bodies.

3. An American Federation of all National and International Trade Unions, to aid and assist each other, to aid and encourage the sale of union-label goods, and to secure national legislation in the interest of the working people and influence public opinion, by peaceful and legal methods, in favor of organized labor.

4. To aid and encourage the labor press of America.

V

EARLY TRIALS OF THE A. F. OF L.

Gompers reveals hardships in maintaining the first headquarters of the American Federation of Labor and the self-sacrifice, not only of himself, but of his family. □ From the book *Seventy Years of Life and Labor* by Samuel Gompers, pp. 271–274. Copyright ©, 1925, by E. P. Dutton & Co., Inc. Renewal, 1952, by Gertrude Cleaves Gompers. Reprinted by permission of the publishers.

The first little office, which was about ten by eight, had a door, a small window, and a brick floor. It was cold in winter and hot in summer. The furniture was make-shift, consisting of a kitchen table brought down from our scanty house furnishings and a box for my chair. My second boy, Henry, who helped me when not in school, and who now takes great pride in the fact that he was the first office boy of the Federation, helped to contrive office furnishings. My daughter, Rose, had a child's writing desk that some-one had given her. Henry took this down to the "office," put legs under it, and nailed it to the wall under the window. Thus equipped, with a box for a seat, Henry was busy during the summer all day long writing wrappers for the paper and doing many errands. He devised files for the office. Just across the street was a grocery store, the friendly proprietor of which contributed empty tomato boxes which Henry transformed into files. Our filing system was very simple. I personally marked each letter, circular, or pamphlet and Henry filed according to the designated subjects. As I was eager for information and had a reverence for the printed word, we soon collected a quantity of valuable information. One essential I had to buy during the first fall was a stove and pipe which cost $8.50. So I managed for a few months.

However, as soon as we had a few pennies we tried to make improvements. We invested one dollar in pine wood and cuttings out of which to construct real files. . . . We were very happy getting conveniences in the office, and when it was all done we felt very rich. It may be hard to understand how genuinely satisfied I was in feeling that I was building something constructive, something that would be helpful, although, of course, I could not foresee the results that were to come. . . . It was some months later, not until October, that I felt wealthy enough to buy a second-hand desk from Hugh McGregor for $2. It is pathetic and tragic to look back over those struggles of the early labor movement, to remember the hardships we endured and the makeshifts that we utilized to develop the labor movement of today. . . .

Money was scarce. There was not always enough for paper and ink. Henry remembers as one of his duties as office boy, going to the school around the corner to borrow a little ink until we could get money to buy a new bottle. Sometimes there was money to pay Henry his three dollars for his week's work, sometimes there was money to pay my week's salary. But whether there was money or not, in the morning we started to work from our home on Sixty-ninth Street and Second Avenue and usually walked to work with our lunch under our arms. If we had ten cents we might ride back—if not we walked. But we did the day's work, ate our sandwich apiece at noon, and got back home when we could. More often than not, it was midnight before I got home—there were meetings, speeches to make, conferences to attend, for the cause of labor is no easy mistress to serve.

In June we had sufficient money to begin publishing the *Trade Union Advocate*. It was a busy period of the month when the paper went to press. I wrote all the copy in long hand and read all the proof. Henry wrote all the wrappers. When the issue was sent round from the printer, Henry and I worked hard at folding and getting the papers ready for the mail. Usually, a few cigarmakers volunteered to help with this work as they were in the same office and could see our difficulties. . . .

I often spent my own money for Federation work rather than stop work because none other was available. There was little enough for all purposes, with a family of eight to be cared for. We had no luxuries—not always the necessaries. Many a time the children had to stay home while shoes or clothes were repaired—there were no changes. When my shoes needed repairing, I wore old slippers in the office while Henry took the shoes over to the shoe shop to be mended before evening. My brother Alexander takes delight in recounting the time when I was going away to a convention, but had no clothes to wear. Finally, after arduous excitement, I succeeded in getting enough to buy a suit.

VI

FUNCTIONS OF TRADE UNIONS

As the American Federation of Labor extended its activity, Gompers developed a philosophy as to the proper role and function of trade unions. His practical aims helped to unify and strengthen the organization. □ From the book *Seventy Years of Life and Labor* by Samuel Gompers, pp. 284–287. Copyright ©, 1925, by E. P. Dutton & Co., Inc. Renewal, 1952, by Gertrude Cleaves Gompers. Reprinted by permission of the publishers.

My earliest official efforts were concentrated in promoting stability of labor organizations. This had to be done by making the idea an inseparable part of the thought and habits of trade unionists by establishing a business basis for unionism and then driving home the fallacy of low dues. Cheap unionism cannot maintain effective economic activity. Sustained office work and paid union officials for administrative work have become the general practice since the Federation was organized. A big service of the Federation has been in crystallizing and unifying labor thought and practice.

To build the Federation we had to secure members. Numbers give confidence not only to members but to outsiders. The membership problem fell into three divisions—affiliation of existing nationals and internationals; chartering of local unions, central bodies, and state federations of labor; when a trade was sufficiently organized we launched a national organization. . . .

A speech I made in Brooklyn in 1887 is typical of the educational work of that time:

The best way to defeat strikes and boycotts is to provide for them. There is no way of decreasing strikes so good as that of making men experienced. From a strong organization generous treatment follows and with fairness on the part of the employer there is no desire to strike or boycott on the part of the men. The best method to decrease strikes is to organize to defend men in the case of strikes. The stronger the union the fewer the strikes. We do not want strikes, but if men are not organized they will have to strike. First, one employer will cut wages, then another, until the rate has fallen so low that the men must strike. We are opposed to sympathetic and foolish strikes. Ignorance is not discipline. It requires more discipline to pay an assessment of $1 a week to help those on strike than to strike in sympathy with them. The first thing a new union does is to want to strike. They overestimate the power of organization without resources. The old unions do not strike, their strength is known. They do not have to strike to resist encroachment. . . .

Economic betterment—today, tomorrow, in home and shop, was the foundation upon which trade unions have been builded. Economic power is the basis upon which may be developed power in other fields. It is the foundation of organized society. Whoever or whatever controls economic power directs and shapes development for the group or the nation. Because I early grasped this fundamental truth, I was never deluded or led astray by rosy theory or fascinating plan that did not square with my fundamental.

VII

THE POLITICAL ROLE OF LABOR

In his report to the 1909 national convention of the A. F. of L., Samuel Gompers included these remarks on the political role of labor. His views mark a sharp departure from tactics of the Knights of Labor. □ *Report of Proceedings of the Twenty-Ninth Annual Convention of the American Federation of Labor,* pp. 32–34. Washington, D.C.: The Law Reporter Printing Co., 1909.

Naturally, during the present year, there has been some lull in the political activities of the country because there has been neither an immediate presidential nor congressional election to stir the minds of the people. The need for adequate remedial, definitive, and protective legislation, both state and national is, however, as great as when I had the honor to submit to you my report a year ago. . . . It was not possible then to ascertain many encouraging facts which have since been verified. We know that at least 6,000,000 votes were cast for the principles espoused by labor. . . .

In 1895 the New York Convention declared:

"That the American Federation of Labor most firmly and unequivocally favors the independent use of the ballot by the trade unionists and workingmen, united regardless of party, that we may elect men from our own ranks to make new laws and administer them along the lines laid down in the legislative demand of the American Federation of Labor, and at the same time secure an impartial judiciary that will not govern us by arbitrary injunctions of the courts, nor act as the pliant tools of corporate wealth.

"That as our efforts are centered against all forms of industrial slavery and economic wrong, we must also direct our utmost energies to remove all forms of political servitude and party slavery to the end that the working people may act as a unit at the polls at every election. . . ."

In accordance with the above instructions I made the following recommendations to the meeting of the Executive Council in April this year and they were endorsed:

"In connection with the subject of legislation, I beg to suggest that inasmuch as there appears to be little disposition on the part of Congress, particularly in its present make-up, to give the relief that we should have from the decision of the Supreme Court of the United States in so far as concerns the Sherman Anti-Trust Law, relief from the abuse of the writ of injunction, or to enact legislation for the extension of the Eight-Hour Law, for the protection of seaman's rights, or for the regulation of convict labor, etc., I recommend that we urge upon organized labor and all reform forces to begin an agitation and to organize so as to be prepared to take action in the next congressional election. . . ."

We must be partisan for a principle and not for a party, but we must make manifest the fact that we have political power and that we intend to use it; otherwise the ballot will become an impotent weapon. Our members and friends can not expect that the officers of the Federation can impress either upon political parties or upon Congress the demands of the workers for justice and right unless those workers themselves have shown sufficient interest in the use of their political power as to make it clear that they are the potent force behind their chosen officers and representatives.

PROBLEM 7

Opposing Views of the
Labor Movement

The struggle between national labor organizations drew the attention of the American press in the late nineteenth century. Of even greater consequence to the history of the United States was the mounting conflict between the ranks of workers and employers. The rapid growth of industry during the second half of the nineteenth century and major changes in the American economic structure created great wealth, but also serious social discord. Sons of American artisans, farmers, and shopkeepers who entered the industrial labor force protested against loss of their "manly independence." They found factory employment to be dull, repetitive, and physically hazardous. Workingmen contended that they were not receiving an equitable share of the wealth they helped to produce.

In response to these problems, many workers turned to labor organizations and strikes in the hope that collective action would provide the remedy for their economic ills.

Workingmen soon discovered that collective efforts to improve economic conditions resulted in the creation of a new set of problems. In the first place, both employers and intellectual leaders tended to be hostile to the activities of trade unions. Practically all employers, and many other well-educated

Americans as well, thought that the demands of labor unions were an infringement on the rights of the factory owners. By the opening years of the twentieth century a vigorous debate on the propriety of labor organizations was under way in the propertied and educated ranks of society. Some corporate executives, like George Baer, denounced labor unions outright. Others, like Marcus A. Hanna, saw in "responsible" trade unions a valuable ally for private enterprise. In addition, there were "progressive" spokesmen who viewed both large business corporations and national labor unions with equal concern.

The diversity of the national groups in the American labor force added to the problems that confronted union organizers. Early trade unions had to forge a sense of common interest among native Americans and newcomers from England, Ireland, and Germany. By the end of the 1880's this formidable task had been partially completed. At that time, however, a new wave of immigration, largely from southern and eastern Europe, began to crest.

The American labor force took on a multinational character. With the arrival of persons whose ways of living were not understood, conflicts among workingmen increased and added to the disputes between workingmen and their employers.

The readings which follow are designed to illustrate the variety of viewpoints on "the labor question." They include opinions which could be found among rank-and-file workers, as well as among businessmen, clergymen, and labor leaders during the years that America was becoming the leading industrial power of the world. As you read, keep in mind the following questions:

1   According to Terence Powderly, how did the nature of the factory system help to stimulate interest among workers in their early attempts to organize labor?

2   Do you agree with George Baer in Reading III that the worker "has no other interest than to secure fair wages"? What "other interests" seem to motivate the striking miner in the second reading?

3   Is Henry Ward Beecher's position well founded on religious grounds? Why?

4   Of the two workers whose views are given in Reading V and in Reading VI, which one would you expect to be most favorable to labor unions? Why?

5   From your reading of the final selection, what characteristic of Samuel Gompers' trade unionism seemed to be most attractive to Marcus Hanna?

I

THE OLD ORDER CHANGES

The impact of the factory system on the American worker in the nine-teenth century is ably described by Terence V. Powderly in his book from which the following selection is taken. ☐ Terence V. Powderly, *Thirty Years of Labor*, pp. 26–27, 30–31. Columbus, Ohio: Excelsior Publishing House, 1890.

With the introduction of machinery, large manufacturing establishments were erected in the cities and towns. Articles that were formerly made by hand, were turned out in large quantities by machinery; prices were lowered, and those who worked by hand found themselves competing with something that could withstand hunger and cold and not suffer in the least. The village blacksmith shop was abandoned, the road-side shoe shop was deserted, the tailor left his bench, and all together these mechanics turned away from their country homes and wended their way to the cities wherein the large factories had been erected. The gates were unlocked in the morning to allow them to enter, and after their daily task was done the gates were closed after them in the evening.

Silently and thoughtfully, these men went to their homes. They no longer carried the keys of the workshop, for workshop, tools and keys belonged not to them, but to their master. Thrown together in this way, in these large hives of industry, men became acquainted with each other, and frequently discussed the question of labor's rights and wrongs. They saw that they no longer were engaged in that competition which is "the life of trade," they realized that it was a competition which ultimately meant death to manhood and independence, unless through some means it became directed into a differ-ent channel. . . .

Competition between man and man is healthy to both, but com-petition between man and the machine is injurious to the former. He who offered to sell his labor after the introduction of machinery, could not hope to compete with a fellow-man in the work he proposed to do; he was forced to compete with a machine, or a whole row of machines, being managed by boys or girls who worked for inadequate wages. With the erection of the factory commenced the combination of capital and capitalists.

Every two, three, ten or fifty men, who united their wealth for the pur-pose of instituting a manufacturing establishment, formed a combination of employers, and to that extent were members of a union whose object was to make profit from the sale of their product, and to secure from other men as much labor as possible, at the lowest rate of compensation.

For one workingman to attempt to successfully compete with a union of that kind was sheerest nonsense; such a thing was, and is, an impossibility. Competition soon took on a double significance; it began to be waged between the men who labored and the men who employed labor. In former times men of equal ability and attainments competed with each other and achieved success, or experienced failure, according to their merits. Beneath the shadow of machinery merit went for naught so far as man's natural ability to perform labor was concerned.

II

STORY OF A COAL MINER

An industry-wide strike of American anthracite miners in 1902 finally led to intervention by President Theodore Roosevelt when mine owners refused to negotiate. The following selection, appearing in *The Independent,* a contemporary magazine, is a miner's reply to the question of why he joined the strike. □ Reprinted with permission of The Free Press of Glencoe from *The American Worker in the Twentieth Century* by Eli Ginzberg and Hyman Berman, pp. 57, 58–61. Copyright © 1963 by The Free Press of Glencoe, A Division of The Macmillan Company.

I am thirty-five years old, married, the father of four children, and have lived in the coal region all my life. Twenty-three of these years have been spent working in and around the mines. My father was a miner. He died ten years ago from "miners' asthma." . . .

In the fifteen years I have worked as a miner I have earned the average rate of wages any of us coal heavers get. Today I am little better off than when I started to do for myself. I have $100 on hand; I am not in debt; I hope to be able to weather the strike without going hungry. . . .

Our daily life is not a pleasant one. When we put on our oil-soaked suit in the morning we can't guess all the dangers which threaten our lives. We walk sometimes miles to the place—to the man way or traveling way, or to the mouth of the shaft on top of the slope. And then we enter the darkened chambers of the mines. On our right and on our left we see the logs that keep up the top and support the sides which may crush us into shapeless masses, as they have done to many of our comrades.

We get old quickly. Powder, smoke, after-damp, bad air—all combine to bring furrows to our faces and asthma to our lungs.

I did not strike because I wanted to; I struck because I had to. A miner —the same as any other workman—must earn fair living wages, or he can't live. And it is not how much you get that counts. It is how much what you get will buy. I have gone through it all, and I think my case is a good sample. . . .

. . . In 1890–91, from June to May, I earned $368.72. That represented eleven months' work, or an average of $33.52 per month. Our rent was $10 per month; store not less than $20. And then I had my oil suits and gum boots to pay for. The result was that after the first year and a half of our married life we were in debt. Not much, of course, and not as much as many of my neighbors, men of larger families, and some who made less money, or in whose case there had been sickness or accident or death. These are all things which a miner must provide for.

I have had fairly good work since I was married. I made the average of what we contract miners are paid; but, as I said before, I am not much better off than when I started.

In 1896 my wife was sick eleven weeks. The doctor came to my house almost every day. He charged me $20 for his services. There was medicine to buy. I paid the drug store $18 in that time. Her mother nursed her, and we kept a girl in the kitchen at $1.50 a week, which cost me $15 for ten weeks, beside the additional living expenses. . . .

Company stores are of the time that has been. Their existence ended two years ago. But we've got a system growing up that threatens to be just as bad. Let me explain. Over a year ago I was given a breast [work area] to drive at one of our mines and was glad to get it. My wife took her cash and went around the different places to buy. When I went to the office for my first pay the "super" [superintendent] met me and asked me if I didn't know his wife's brother George kept a store. I answered "Yes," and wanted to know what that had to do with it.

"Nothing, only I thought I'd call your attention to it," he answered.

No more was said then. But the next day I got a quiet tip that my breast was to be abandoned. This set me thinking. I went to the boss and after a few words, told him my wife had found brother-in-law George's store and that she liked it much better than where she had bought before. I told him the other store didn't sell the right kind of silk waists, and their patent leather shoes were away back. Brother-in-law George had the right kind of stuff and, of course, we were willing to pay a few cents more to get just what we wanted.

That was sarcastic, but it's the cash that has the influence. I have had work at that colliery ever since. I know my living costs me from 10 to 15 per cent extra. But I kept my job. . . .

Our condition can be no worse: it might and must be better. The luxuries of the rich we do not ask; we do not want butter for our bread and meat for our soup. We do not want silk and laces for our wives and daughters. But we want to earn enough to buy them a clean calico once in a while. Our boys are not expecting automobiles and membership cards in clubs of every city, but they want their fathers to earn enough to keep them at school until they have a reasonably fair education.

III

GOD PROTECTS THE WORKINGMAN

As may be seen in the following newspaper account, George Baer, president of the Philadelphia and Reading Railroad Company, viewed the anthracite strike quite differently from the miner who was quoted in the previous reading. Baer's railroad controlled the most important anthracite coal mines in the nation. □ *The New York Times*, August 21, 1902. Copyright © 1902 by The New York Times Company.

WILKESBARRE, PENN., Aug. 20.—W. F. Clark, a photographer of this city, recently addressed a letter to President Baer of the Philadelphia and Reading Railroad Company, appealing to him as a Christian to settle the miners' strike. The writer said if Christ was taken more into our business affairs there would be less trouble in the world, and that if Mr. Baer granted the strikers a slight concession they would gladly return to work and the President of the Philadelphia and Reading would have the blessing of God and the respect of the nation.

President Baer replied as follows:

"I see you are evidently biased in your religious views in favor of the right of the working man to control a business in which he has no other interest than to secure fair wages for the work he does. I beg of you not to be discouraged. The rights and interests of the laboring man will be protected and cared for, not by the labor agitators, but by the Christian men to whom God in His infinite wisdom has given the control of the property interests of the country. Pray earnestly that the right may triumph, always remembering that the Lord God Omnipotent still reigns and that His reign is one of law and order, and not of violence and crime."

IV

SERMONS AGAINST STRIKERS

The coal strike of 1902 was not the first to draw national attention to the question of labor unions. Strikes had become commonplace in American life since the 1850's, and in 1877 the most extensive walkout of the century took place. This great work stoppage involved all of the trunk railroad lines of the country and included thousands of nonrailroad workers who joined in sympathy. Federal troops were finally dispatched to control the strikers after President Hayes declared a "state of insurrection." These events inspired sermons by the Reverend Henry Ward Beecher in July 1877 condemning the actions of the strikers. The selections which follow are news reports of the sermons. □ *The New York Times,* July 23, 1877. Copyright © 1877 by The New York Times Company.

Plymouth Church was crowded last evening by a large audience, and Mr. Beecher in the course of his discourse alluded to the great railroad strike. He said that disorder had broken out all along the great roads of several portions of the country, and riots of an unusual magnitude had taken place.

This Sabbath day was not, he said, one of stillness, for there were military movements throughout the land, and from their city soldiers were being dispatched to quell the riots. . . . Such outbreaks . . . sprang from ignorance and passion. Such riots arose because their promoters and those who abetted them were ignorant of political economy. The question of labor and capital was a question of citizenship and of corporate life. He proceeded to eulogize the working classes, and dwelt particularly on the industry, sobriety, and heroism of the railroad employees, and pointed out the necessity for harmonious working together of the laborer and the capitalist. . . . He then said:

"What right had the working men, the members of those great organizations, to say to any one, 'You shall not work for wages which we refuse.' They had a perfect right to say to the employers, 'We shall not work for you,' but they had no right to tyrannize over their fellowmen. They had put themselves in an attitude of tyrannical opposition to all law and order and they could not be defended. The necessities of the great railroad companies demanded that there should be a reduction of wages. There must be continual shrinkage until things come back to the gold standard, and wages, as well as greenbacks, provisions and property, must share in it. It was true that $1 a day was not enough to support a man and five children, if a man would insist on smoking and drinking beer. Was not a dollar a day enough to buy bread? Water costs nothing. (Laughter.) Men cannot live by bread, it is true; but the man who cannot live on bread and water is not fit to live. (Laughter.) When a man is educated away from the power of self-denial, he is falsely educated. A family may live on good bread and water in the morning, water and bread at midday, and good water and bread at night. (Continued laughter.) Such may be called the bread of affliction, but it was fit that man should eat of the bread of affliction. Thousands would be very glad of a dollar a day, and it added to the sin of the men on strike for them to turn and say to those men, 'You can do so, but you shall not.' There might be special cases of hardship, but the great laws of political economy could not be set at defiance." He concluded by declaring that in the end, the men on strike would be defeated, trade resumed, and prosperity once more reign throughout the land. (Applause.).

A week later the Reverend Beecher added the following warning against American adoption of "European notions." □ *The New York Times,* July 29, 1877. Copyright © 1877 by The New York Times Company.

We look upon the importation of the communistic and like European notions as abominations. Their notions and theories that the Government should be paternal and take care of the welfare of its subjects and provide them with labor, is un-American. It is the form in which oppression has had its most disastrous scope in the world. The American doctrine is that it is the duty of the Government merely to protect the people while they are taking care of themselves—nothing more than that. "Hands off," we say to the Government; "see to it that we are protected in our rights and our individuality. No more than that." The theories of Europe in regard to the community of property we reject because they are against natural law and will never be practicable. God has intended the great to be great and the little to be little. No equalization process can ever take place until men are made equal as productive forces. It is a wild vision, not a practicable theory. The European theories of combinations between workmen and trade-unions and communes destroy the individuality of the person, and there is no possible way of preserving the liberty of the people except by the maintenance of individual liberty, intact from Government and intact from individual meddling. Persons have the right to work when or where they please, as long as they please, and for what they please, and any attempt to infringe on this right, and to put good workmen on a level with poor workmen—any such attempt to regiment labor is preposterous.

V

STORY OF A STEELWORKER

In 1910 the Russell Sage Foundation, a private research organization, conducted an extensive survey of conditions in the steel industry, which was then almost totally nonunionized. The selection below is taken from that survey and represents the outlook of an "Old Immigrant" from northern Europe on working conditions. Note his attitude toward fellow workers from the class of "New Immigrants" who came from southern and eastern Europe. □ John A. Fitch, *The Steel Workers*, pp. 11–12. New York: Russell Sage Foundation, Copyright © 1911.

John Griswold is a Scotch-Irish furnace boss who came to America and got a laborer's position at a Pittsburgh blast furnace when the common labor force was largely Irish. Those were the days before the advent of the "furriners." I sat in Griswold's sitting room in his four-room cottage one evening and he told me about the men who work at the furnaces. . . .

"Mighty few men have stood what I have, I can tell you. I've been twenty years at the furnaces and been workin' a twelve-hour day all that time, seven days in the week. We go to work at seven in the mornin' and we get through at night at six. We work that way for two weeks and then we work the long turn and change to the night shift of thirteen hours. The long turn is when we go on at seven Sunday mornin' and work through the whole twenty-four hours up to Monday mornin'. That puts us onto the night turn for the next two weeks, and the other crew onto the day. The next time they get the long turn and we get twenty-four hours off, but it don't do us much good. I get home at about half past seven Sunday mornin' and go to bed as soon as I've had breakfast. I get up about noon so as to get a bit o' Sunday to enjoy, but I'm tired and sleepy all the afternoon. Now, if we had eight hours it would be different. I'd start to work, say, at six and I'd be done at two and I'd come home, and after dinner me and the missus could go to the park if we wanted to, or I could take the childer to the country where there ain't any saloons. That's the danger,—the childer runnin' on the streets and me with no time to take them any place else. That's what's driven the Irish out of the industry. It ain't the Hunkies, [Hungarians or other eastern European workers]—they couldn't do it,—but the Irish don't have to work this way. There was fifty of them here with me sixteen years ago and now where are they? I meet 'em sometimes around the city, ridin' in carriages and all of them wearin' white shirts, and here I am with these Hunkies. They don't seem like men to me hardly. They can't talk United States. You tell them something and they just look and say 'Me no fustay, [understand] me no fustay,' that's all you can get out of 'em. And I'm here with them all the time, twelve hours a day and every day and I'm all alone,—not a mother's son of 'em that I can talk to. Everybody says I'm a fool to stay here,—I dunno, mebbe I am. . . ."

VI

AN IMMIGRANT SPEAKS

A "New Immigrant" told his own story to a reporter from *The Independent* in 1904. His narrative illustrates the problems of an immigrant in his adjustment to American life. □ Reprinted with permission of The Free Press of Glencoe from *The American Worker in the Twentieth Century* by Eli Ginzberg and Hyman Berman, pp. 47–48, 49–50, 51. Copyright © 1963 by The Free Press of Glencoe, A Division of The Macmillan Company.

Soon after my arrival in this country, I knew that money was everything I needed. My money was almost gone and I thought that I would soon die unless I got a job, for this was not like home. Here money was everything and a man without money must die.

One morning my friends woke me up at five o'clock and said, "Now if you want life, liberty and happiness," they laughed, "you must push for yourself. You must get a job. Come with us." And we went to the [stock] yards. . . . We went to the doors of one big slaughter house. There was a crowd of about 200 men waiting there for a job. They looked hungry and kept watching the door. At last a special policeman came out and began pointing to men, one by one. Each one jumped forward. Twenty-three were taken. Then they all went inside and all the others turned their faces away and looked tired. I remember one boy sat down and cried, just next to me, on a pile of boards. Some policemen waved their clubs and we all walked on. . . .

That night I told my friends that I would not do this many days, but would go some place else. "Where?" they asked me, and I began to see then that I was in bad trouble, because I spoke no English. Then one man told me to give him $5 to give the special policeman. I did this and the next morning the policeman pointed me out, so I had a job. I have heard some big talk since then about my American freedom of contract, but I do not think I had much freedom in bargaining for this job with the Meat Trust. My job was in the cattle killing room. I pushed the blood along the gutter. . . .

I held this job six weeks and then I was turned off. I think some other man had paid for my job, or perhaps I was too slow. The foreman in that room wanted quick men to make the work rush, because he was paid more if the work was done cheaper and quicker. . . .

. . . At last I had a chance to help myself. Summer was over and Election Day was coming. The Republican boss in our district, Jonidas, was a saloonkeeper. A friend took me there. Jonidas shook hands and treated me fine. He taught me to sign my name, and the next week I went with him to an office and signed some paper, and then I could vote. I voted as I was told, and then they got me back into the yards to work, because one big politician owns stock in one of those houses. Then I felt that I was getting in beside the game. I was in a combine like other sharp men. Even when work was slack I was all right, because they got me a job in the street cleaning department. . . . All of us were telling our friends to come soon. Soon they came—even thousands. The employers in the yard like this, because those sharp foremen are inventing new machines and the work is easier to learn, and so these slow Lithuanians and even green girls can learn to do it, and then the Americans and Germans and Irish are put out and the employer saves money, because the Lithuanians work cheaper. This was why the American labor unions began to organize us all just the same as they had organized the Bohemians and Poles before us. . . .

. . . I joined the Cattle Butchers' Union. This union is honest and it has done me a great deal of good.

It has raised my wages. The man who worked at my job before the union came was getting through the year an average of $9 a week. I am getting $11. In my first job I got $5 a week. The man who works there now gets $5.75.

It has given me more time to learn to read and speak and enjoy life like an American. I never work now from 6 A.M. to 9 P.M. and then be idle the next day. I work now from 7 A.M. to 5:30 P.M., and there are not so many idle days. The work is evened up. . . .

The union is doing another good thing. It is combining all the nationalities. The night I joined the Cattle Butchers' Union I was led into the room by a Negro member. With me were Bohemians, Germans, and Poles, and Mike Donnelly, the President, is an Irishman. He spoke to us in English and then three interpreters told us what he said. We swore to be loyal to our union above everything else except the country, the city and the State—to be faithful to each other—to protect the women workers—to do our best to understand the history of the labor movement, and to do all we could to help it on. . . .

But the best thing the union does is to make me feel more independent. I do not have to pay to get a job and I cannot be discharged unless I am no good. For almost the whole 30,000 men and women are organized now in some of our unions and they all are directed by our central council. No man knows what it means to be sure of his job unless he has been fired like I was once without any reason being given.

So this is why I joined the labor union. . . . There are thousands of immigrants like me. Over 300,000 immigrants have been organized in the last three years by the American Federation of Labor. . . . You must get money to live well, and to get money you must combine. I cannot bargain alone with the Meat Trust. I tried it and it does not work.

VII

VIEW FROM THE MIDDLE OF THE ROAD

Marcus A. Hanna was the head of one of the largest coal and coke companies in the nation. He was also a major power in the Republican party and became a United States Senator in 1902. As president of the National Civic Federation, an organization interested in improvement of labor-management relations, he took a conciliatory attitude toward industrial problems. ☐ Marcus A. Hanna, "Industrial Conciliation and Arbitration," *The Annals of the American Academy of Political and Social Science,* Vol. 20, July-December 1902, pp. 21, 25–26. Philadelphia: American Academy of Political and Social Science, copyright © 1902.

To have success in conciliation, or arbitration, there must be thorough effective organization on both sides. The large aggregations of capital, feared at first by labor, may prove to be labor's best friend, in that, control of a trade being thus centralized, there is opportunity to establish friendly relations which shall make uniform conditions throughout the country, or large sections thereof, and reduce the basis of competition to the quality of the product rather than to the concessions forced from labor. . . .

My experience has taught me, my friends, that the employer because of his position has the most to do, and it must be expected that the employers, at least in the beginning of this educational work, should go more than half way. They provide work, and are responsible for the conduct of business, and upon them rests the responsibility of seeing that the men receive their share of its benefits. We must rise to a higher level, where we can have a broader view of this question, where we can tear ourselves away from the prejudices which have heretofore stood between capital and labor.

I believe in organized labor, and I have for thirty years. I believe in it because it is a demonstrated fact that where the concerns and interests of labor are entrusted to able and honest leadership, it is much easier for those who represent the employers to come into close contact with the laborer, and, by dealing with fewer persons, to accomplish results quicker and better.

The trusts have come to stay. Organized labor and organized capital are but forward steps in the great industrial evolution that is taking place. We would just as soon think of going back to primitive methods of manufacturing as we would primitive methods of doing business, and it is our duty, those of us who represent the employers, from this time on to make up our minds that this question is one that must be heard.

You are well aware that there has been a tendency in this country, from the very nature of things, to what is called socialism. . . . There is no question concerning our body politic to-day that should command deeper or more serious thought. There is nothing in the organization of society in this country that can afford to permit the growth of socialistic ideas. They are un-American and unnatural to us as a people.

In the beginning of this work I received great encouragement from an address which Samuel Gompers [President of the American Federation of Labor] made in Cooper Union Institute, in New York, about a year and a half ago, when he took the broad ground that in the interests of labor there was no room for the socialist or the anarchist, no room for men who undertook to disturb the principles of our society and government. When such words came from a man leading the largest labor organization in the world, a man of advanced thought and of honest intent, I knew that now is the time to strike, now is the time to proclaim to the American people that in the consideration of this question, which sooner or later must be forced upon us, we must consider what is for the best interests of society as well as for our material development.

PROBLEM 8

The Industrial Workers
of the World

The collapse of the Knights of Labor did not extinguish interest among unorganized workers for an industrial union to represent the demands of the unskilled. These workers were handicapped by lack of real weapons to force concessions from bosses who could easily replace them by strike-breakers, called scabs. Since the A.F. of L. made few efforts to organize the unskilled, most of the union activity of the latter was confined to spontaneous strikes, often accompanied by violence and usually unsuccessful in gaining the strikers' objectives. It was not until enactment in the 1930's of the Wagner Act, changing the bargaining situation by requiring employers to negotiate with elected representatives of their employees, that most unskilled workers were able to organize in the United States.

Between 1905 and 1917 the idea of industrial unionism was kept alive by a radical movement enlisting socialists, anarchists, and the members of several national unions, most important of which was the Western Federation of Miners. These elements combined to form the Industrial Workers of the World (I.W.W.), or "Wobblies" as they came to be known. Within a few years of the founding of the I.W.W. at Chicago in 1905, the socialists withdrew because of their reluctance to abandon the ballot box as a principal means of achieving workers' aims. The I.W.W. remained devoted to direct action, which meant strikes, sabotage, and demonstrations of various sorts.

For more than a decade news of the I.W.W. filled newspapers and periodicals throughout the nation. The Wobblies were strongest among the lumber workers, miners, and itinerant harvest hands of the West and South. Between 1912 and 1914 they invaded the East, where they staged spectacular strikes, particularly among formerly unorganized textile workers, most of whom were recent immigrants. Once the excitement of a strike was over, talk of revolution and of sabotage frightened the conservative immigrants, and I.W.W. locals lost members in a steady stream. Western states passed laws that ruled against activities of syndicalists, or those who would overthrow any form of state. Thus, the I.W.W. was outlawed in the West. The final blow to the union occurred when federal government officials arrested I.W.W. leaders and closed the union offices on charges of subversion. Although the I.W.W. continued to exist on paper, its power was broken during World War I. Today it has only a few members in scattered locals.

The I.W.W. represents a response by a specific group of workers to a specific set of economic, social, and political conditions. In the 1830's most union members expended more effort in political activity than in trade union work. With the formation of the A.F. of L., the skilled workers began to struggle for definite economic gains for themselves. Neither of these alternatives was open to the Wobblies. Most of them did not have the franchise. Most of them lacked the skill essential for gaining bargaining power with their employers. Yet they faced serious problems which demanded immediate attention. The solutions they proposed grew out of the social and economic setting in which the members of the I.W.W. lived and worked.

Problem 8 consists of two readings. The first is the preamble to the I.W.W. constitution, which sets forth in brief form the revolutionary philosophy of the Wobblies. The second is an article by Robert W. Bruère which places the Wobbly movement in its setting. As you read them, think about the following questions:

1   What basic attitude toward American society is implied by the preamble to the I.W.W. constitution?

2   What sort of men joined the Wobblies? Were they typical American workers?

3   What were the working conditions under which most I.W.W. members labored? How were these conditions related to the type of men who joined the Wobblies? to I.W.W. philosophy?

4   To what, and to whom, does the author of Reading II attribute the growth of the radical labor movement?

I

THE PHILOSOPHY OF THE I.W.W.

The best exposition of the philosophy of the I.W.W. is contained in the preamble to the I.W.W. constitution. The version of the preamble which appears below was written after the socialists left the organization. It expresses the position of the itinerant harvest hands and lumber workers who dominated the I.W.W. after 1908. □ P. F. Brissenden, *The I.W.W.: A Study of American Syndicalism,* pp. 351–352. New York: Columbia University Press, copyright © 1920.

The working class and the employing class have nothing in common. There can be no peace so long as hunger and want are found among millions of working people and the few, who make up the employing class, have all the good things of life. . . .

Between these two classes a struggle must go on until the workers of the world organize as a class, take possession of the earth and the machinery of production and abolish the wage system.

We find that the centering of management of industries into fewer and fewer hands makes the trade unions unable to cope with the ever-growing power of the employing class. The trade unions foster a state of affairs which allows one set of workers to be pitted against another set of workers in the same industry, thereby helping defeat one another in wage wars. Moreover, the trade unions aid the employing class to mislead the workers into the belief that the workers have interest in common with their employers.

These conditions can be changed and the interest of the working class upheld only by an organization formed in such a way that all its members in any one industry, or in all industries if necessary, cease work whenever a strike or lockout is on in any department thereof, thus making an injury to one an injury to all.

Instead of the conservative motto, "A fair day's wage for a fair day's work," we must inscribe on our banner the revolutionary watchword, "Abolition of the wage system." It is the historic mission of the working class to do away with capitalism. The army of production must be organized, not only for the every-day struggle with capitalists, but to carry on production when capitalism shall have been overthrown. By organizing industrially we are forming the structure of the new society within the shell of the old.

II

AN INTERPRETATION OF THE I.W.W.

Following the Lawrence, Massachusetts textile strike in 1912, a number of sensational articles about the I.W.W. began to appear in magazines and newspapers. Writers accused I.W.W. members of an amazing variety of crimes against society. Few authors tried to see the problems and activities of the Wobblies against the setting which had provoked them. To counteract some of the more sensational articles, Robert W. Bruère wrote the analysis of the I.W.W. which follows. □ Robert W. Bruère, "The Industrial Workers of the World," *Harper's Magazine*, July 1918, pp. 250–252, 253, 254, 255–256, 257.

The Industrial Workers of the World are most numerous among the migratory workers of the West; among the homeless, wayfaring men who follow the harvests from Texas across the Canadian border; among the lumberjacks who pack their quilts from camp to distant camp in the fir and pine and spruce forests of the Northwest; and among the metalliferous miners of Michigan, Minnesota, Montana, Idaho, Colorado, Arizona, and Old Mexico. In other words, they are strongest among the men upon whom the nation depends for three of its basic raw materials—materials of fundamental importance at all times; of crucial importance in time of war.

According to our best information, approximately four-fifths of these migratory workers are men whose family ties have been broken —"womanless, voteless, and jobless men." Competent authorities estimate that about one-half of them are native Americans, and the other half men who have been uprooted by labor-brokers and padrones from their native ethnic and social environments; voluntary or forced immigrants from the agricultural districts of Ireland, from the Welsh and Cornish mines, from the hungry hills of Italy, Serbia, Greece, and Turkish Asia Minor. . . .

The division superintendent of a great Western railroad recently explained to me his reluctant part in the creation of the socially disintegrating conditions out of which the migratory workers and the rebellious propaganda of the I.W.W. have sprung.

"The men down East," he said, "the men who have invested their money in our road, measure our administrative efficiency by money return—by net earnings and dividends. Many of our shareholders have never seen the country our road was built to serve; they get their impression of it and of its people, not from living contact with men, but from the impersonal ticker. They judge us by quotations and the balance-sheet.

"The upshot is that we have to keep expenses cut close as a jailbird's hair. Take such a detail as the maintenance of ways, for example—the upkeep of tracks and road-beds. This work should be going on during the greater part of the year. But to keep costs down, we have crowded it into four months.

"It is impossible to get the number and quality of men we need by the offer of a four months' job. So we publish advertisements . . . that read something like this: 'MEN WANTED! HIGH WAGES! PERMANENT EMPLOYMENT!' We know when we put our money into these advertisements that they are—well, part of a pernicious system of sabotage. We know that we are not going to give permanent employment. But we lure men with false promises, and they come.

"At the end of four months we lay them off, strangers in a strange country, many of them thousands of miles from their old homes. We wash our hands of them. They come with golden dreams, expecting in many cases to build homes, rear families, become substantial American citizens. After a few weeks, their savings gone, the single men grow restless and start moving; a few weeks more and the married men bid their families good-by. They take to the road hunting for jobs, planning to send for their families when they find steady work. Some of them swing onto the freight-trains and beat their way to the nearest town, are broke when they get there, find the labor market over-supplied, and, as likely as not, are thrown into jail as vagrants. Some of them hit the trail for the woods, the ranches, and the mines. Many of them never find a stable anchorage again; they become hobos, vagabonds, wayfarers—migratory and intermittent workers, outcasts from society and the industrial machine, ripe for the denationalized fellowship of the I.W.W."

This is a small but characteristic example of a vast system of human exploitation that has been developed by the powerful suction of our headlong industrial expansion, by the Gargantuan growth of our steel and packing industries, of our logging operations from Florida to the Pacific coast, of our feverish railroad and mining enterprises. Even in ordinary times these gold-brick [dishonest] advertisements are posted not only in the labor market of our great cities, but also in the distant agricultural and mountain villages across the sea. For generations the hustling builders of American wealth have recruited men from all corners of the earth without regard to their adaptability to American life, and without any planned provision for their transformation into American citizens. They come to Ellis Island and other Atlantic and Pacific ports and are there labeled and transhipped like freight to vaguely apprehended destinations. During its recent investigation of labor disturbances in the Arizona copper country, the President's Mediation Commission found as many as thirty-two different nationalities represented in a single mining-camp. In the great mining city of Butte, Montana, one of the wealthiest sources of copper and of precious metals in the world, I recently found a score of alien tongues, but not so much as one night school for the teaching of English to foreigners. In the vast regions traveled by the migratory workers, especially in the states where prohibition has abolished the saloon, practically the only social refuge where these strangers are welcomed and made to feel at home is the union hall, and in the lumber and agricultural districts it is almost exclusively the I.W.W. headquarters.

In approaching any consideration of the I.W.W. as a labor movement striving toward industrial revolution, it is of the first importance to remember that the organization is not an exotic, but a perfectly natural, product of conditions for which we, as a self-governing democracy, are ourselves responsible. We must not allow ourselves to be diverted from the actual conditions which have produced this movement by the highly colored and frequently extravagant language in which the members of the I.W.W. have expressed their protest. I dwell upon these facts because the background of the great migratory labor group out of which the I.W.W. is principally recruited is filled in by our antiquated immigration policy and our anarchistic habits of labor distribution. As a community we can no more protect ourselves by denunciations and indictments of the I.W.W. based on their tracts and speeches, than we can keep ourselves from communicable diseases by punishing sick men for their fevered utterances. . . .

The case of Bisbee, where twelve hundred strikers and their alleged sympathizers who had committed no violence were snatched from their homes and deported at the muzzles of guns into the desert of New Mexico, is notorious. But it is no more noteworthy than scores of less widely heralded instances. In one of the Northwestern states there is a comparatively small mining-camp whose economic and social setting runs true to type. Its population has been recruited in the traditional fashion; it has the usual sharp division between propertyowners and propertyless men, between the masters and the strangers in the house. A strike broke out there last summer, brought on by the igniting friction of the rising cost of living upon an accumulation of old estrangements and grievances. Among the strikers were a number of Finns. When the selective draft law went into effect, certain of these Finnish strikers failed to register. This gave the best citizens, the men of property, a dignified vent for their repressed resentments and animosities. Organized as a liberty committee or loyalty league, the currently approved designation for vigilantes, armed and raising the cry of treason, they descended upon the Finnish community, herded some seventy-five of the strikers together, placed them on a special train, and deported them to the nearest town with a jail large enough to hold them.

The alleged offense was a violation of a Federal statute. A government official of the district went to the jail to see what kind of game the vigilantes had bagged for him. He found that most of the prisoners neither spoke nor understood English and that the liberty committee had not taken the trouble to interpret the Draft Act to them. They had a dazed idea that they were to have been summarily torn from their families and friends and sent to the trenches to fight for Russia. When the law was interpreted they expressed their unanimous readiness to serve the United States in any capacity the official might indicate, although they did hope they might serve somewhere in America. The official's investigation, corroborated by a previous investigation made on the ground by a Secret Service agent, revealed no international or premeditated violation of the Federal statute. He decided that, as a preliminary to the straightening out of the misunderstanding, the men should be restored to their homes. When he announced this decision, one of the leaders of the liberty committee protested that if the strikers were brought back to the camp he would tear up his Liberty Bonds and forswear further service to the government of the United States.

Nevertheless, the strikers were returned to their homes and after a brief interval the liberty committee descended upon the Finnish community again, seized certain alleged "agitators," charged them with being members of the I.W.W., and threw them into jail. . . .

It is in these communities which are simplified to one industry centering about some precious raw material, and not in the complex manufacturing centers, that the two classes are brought face to face, and the class struggle which is latent in a more complex social organization lies perpetually on the surface. These facts, emphasized by the violence and peculiar bitterness growing out of such incidents as that of the Finnish community, are undoubtedly the direct inspiration of the opening dogma of the I.W.W. preamble. . . .

The administrative practices which grow out of such situations of abnormal psychological tension are probably the immediate incentive to the peculiar strategy and tactics associated with the I.W.W.—"the strike on the job" and "the conscientious withdrawal of efficiency," phrases used by the I.W.W. as lay substitutes for what is technically known as "sabotage," the habit of going about one's work with a heavy foot, as do men who wear wooden shoes, running the human machine at low speed after the manner of manufacturers in the off season.

Because of the vulnerable character of the mines and the open woods, it is customary to keep them guarded by Secret Service men who readily degenerate into spies. I know mining-camps where the local managers keep secret agents on watch over the foremen; where the foremen bribe men to spy upon their fellow-workmen down in the mines; and where the absentee owners in the East employ detectives to report on the managers. It is not an uncommon thing to find officers of the wage-workers' organization in the pay of the company, while the wage-workers in turn have clandestine channels of information running into the inner executive offices of their employers. All this weird machinery of espionage is greatly extended in times of threatened or actual industrial disturbance. It is supplemented by a "rustling card" or blacklisting system by means of which "agitators" can be followed from one end of the country to the other. There is no doubt that the so-called *agent provocateur* had a hand in fomenting the strikes that recently spread like an epidemic from Butte in Montana to Bisbee on the Mexican border. He is one of the tools used to foment suspicion and dissension among the men when they show a disposition to cohesiveness and mass action. All these things give rise to what, for lack of a more precise term, one may call a "stool-pigeon psychology"—a mental state characterized by haunting fears and suppressed terror, such as prevailed in Russia under the old régime.

This atmosphere is not conducive to open democratic organization of the type conventionally advocated by the recognized unions of the American Federation of Labor. These unions, with their highly centralized craft organizations, have been notably unsuccessful in reaching the migratory workers. In times of large labor surplus when a disaffected worker, spotted by the furtive eye of the "stool-pigeon," could be conveniently replaced with an imported immigrant, even the I.W.W. has been outwitted and balked in its attempts to establish a bond of solidarity among the hobo miners and the wayfaring lumberjacks. But its comparatively decentralized form of organization has proved better adapted to this purpose than the centralized organization of the older union. And the shutting of the floodgates of immigration by the war has greatly increased the effectiveness of the so-called "intermittent strike" and "strike on the job." This is how the thing works. Demands for improved conditions, higher wages, shorter hours, participation in the discipline and government of the working force, are made by the men and turned down by the employers. A strike is called—and broken. The men return to work, but the strike is not "called off." It is only carried into the stronghold of the "enemy," like the guerrilla warfare waged by a conquered people.

Last summer the I.W.W. called a strike in the Northwestern woods after their demands for an eight-hour day, better food, and more sanitary bunkhouses had been ignored by the officials of the lumber companies. These demands were formulated a month before our declaration of war against Germany. The strike went into effect. Rather than concede the eight-hour day on the demand of an "outlaw organization," and in spite of appeals from the Governor of Washington and the Secretary of War for the inauguration of the eight-hour day on patriotic grounds, the operators fell back on their reserve capital and permitted their plants to run down. When the strike was on the point of failure through the starvation of the workers, the I.W.W. decided to return to work, but with muscles and wits geared to an eight-hour speed in the ten-hour camps or mills. They resorted to all manner of cunning devices to accomplish their purpose. "Playing the Hoosier" was one of them.

"When you go up into the camp today," a lumberjack said to me, "you'll find a spar tree in the middle of the workings with steel cables running out into the woods to bring the logs down to the skidway. Running along the skidway you'll see other cables running from the donkey-engine up to the choker-chain; well, every now and then one of those cables snaps. When everything is running right, when the men are satisfied with their working conditions, you'd see a half-dozen men—every man within call—jumping in and splicing that cable. But when you are striking on the job and a cable snaps, you just stand there and play the Hoosier; you don't know anything more about splicing than a yokel, and you wait until the boss finds the man who is paid to do that particular job. Before repairs are made a half-hour is gone—three-quarters of an hour—an hour! Say, it's easy to do eight hours' work on a ten hours' job; all you've got to do is play the Hoosier! Practise conscientious withdrawal of efficiency! Fold your arms and look innocent!"

"But what of criminal sabotage," I asked, "what of spikes in the logs to smash the saw? What of emery in the lubricating oil? What of phosphorus balls in the woods?"

"Say, friend," said he, "what would we be putting spikes in the logs for? Would we be aiming to kill our fellow-workers at the saw—or any one else, for that matter? And as for the mills and the woods, won't we be taking them over one of these days, and what sense would there be in destroying what is going to belong to us? All we aim to destroy is the parasite's profits, and the wage system; the plant—say, we want that to be all there, and as fine as you can make it against the time when the revolution will give birth to the new society out of the old!"

That is their great dream, the pot of gold at the end of their rainbow—the new society in which those who are now "wage slaves" will own and operate the great nationalized and internationalized industry—in which all of the industries will be bound together under the government of the O. B. U.—the One Big Union—the International Industrial Commonwealth. . . .

. . . [The] constitution of the I.W.W. embodies their feeling that the government, which our political democracy has established, has failed the workers. They feel that the modern "capitalistic state" is powerless to safeguard their interests, and that their only hope is to conquer and operate the basic industries and so create an industrial state based upon the democratic representation of a nationalized and internationalized industry owned and operated by the workers themselves.

Most of us look for the ultimate democratization of industry through the slow process of social and political evolution, and this I.W.W. demand for a new state on the ground that the present state is not a democracy shocks our sensibility and moves us to shout "treason." But the other side of the industrial controversy is doing in effect exactly the same thing. The representatives of the copper companies, for example, asserted after the Bisbee deportation that they ignored the State and Federal authorities and acted upon a law of their own making, because they could not trust the government to take action which, in their private judgment, was necessary; because the present state was powerless to safeguard their interests. Both sides feel that the state has failed them and that they are, therefore, at liberty to defy it and to subvert its laws.

The blame belongs primarily on the indifferent and ignorant public which has allowed this situation to grow up between classes of its citizens; which has not apprehended democracy as something wider than the right to vote. It is the failure of public opinion, of your opinion and mine. It is against us that the I.W.W. strives to establish a new state. It is our laws that the employers disregard.

What I have written is not by way of palliation of the acts either of the I.W.W. or of the men who operate big business. It is, rather, an explanation of the growth and power of the Industrial Workers of the World, an institution springing up because of the unhealthy soil we have permitted to accumulate in the fields of our great basic industries, and grown straight from the seeds of business lawlessness and the exploitation of our immigrant population. It is no time to blame any one but ourselves for having failed to adopt a public policy based on even-handed justice to all men, and under which private interests will be subordinated to all public advantage. The rebellious spirit of the I.W.W. propaganda is essentially an expression of antisocial conditions for which we, as citizens of a democratic nation, are ourselves responsible. It points to one of the factors which must be taken into account in the period of political, social, and industrial reconstruction which the cumulative pressure of the war has brought to our doors.

The Great Steel Strike of 1919

From September 1919 until January 1920 the steel industry was the scene of one of the most bitterly fought strikes in the history of the United States.

The conflict climaxed a wave of violence accompanying the readjustment of the economy after World War I. The birth in Russia of the Communist International, the world-wide Marxist organization devoted to the overthrow of the capitalist system, coincided with these disturbances. Many Americans, among them influential government officials, connected the two events. Consequently, the postwar strikes took place in an atmosphere of hysteria and violence.

Two crucial developments set the stage for the steel strike. The first was the establishment of a new union organization. Since the 1890's the craft unions, particularly the Amalgamated Association of Iron, Steel and Tin Workers, had found it impossible to negotiate with a huge modern steel company such as the United States Steel Corporation. The need to coordinate the efforts of twenty-four separate unions, each claiming jurisdiction, complicated matters for A.F. of L. leaders who rejected the idea of industrial unionism.

Immediately after the war a single National Committee for Organizing Iron and Steel Workers was created by the A. F. of L. to gain the support of all workers in the industry. The steel magnates, already chafing under government-imposed collective bargaining during the war, made up their minds to resist to the bitter end.

The second development was the changing role of the federal government. During the war the government had encouraged collective bargaining in the hope of stabilizing production and avoiding costly strikes. Labor had come to look upon the federal government as a possible ally in its drive to bring the steel executives to the bargaining table. Furthermore, high wartime wages had encouraged steel workers to believe that favorable conditions would continue and that further gains would be forthcoming. Steelworkers hoped particularly to eliminate the twelve-hour day and the seven-day week. The termination of war contracts, however, removed the government as a factor in negotiations, leaving the unions to contend with powerful magnates alone. Indeed, when violence broke out, federal troops were often employed to help the owners break strikes.

The Great Steel Strike of 1919 grew out of this confused social setting. It provides an excellent case study of the numerous forces involved in a nation-wide work stoppage. The strike reveals the action and interaction of workers, employers, government, the public, the press, and many other important elements of American life. The loss of the strike helps to explain why workers turned from craft organizations to industrial unionism in the 1930's.

The selections which follow are all drawn from contemporary sources. They capture the spirit and flavor of the time. As you read, consider these questions:

1 What significance (if any) do you see in the fact that the right of collective bargaining appears first in the list of demands in Reading I? What other issues did the strikers stress?

2 Are the newspaper accounts of the steel strike objective? Explain your viewpoint.

3 Why did the strikers lose? What role did the nature of their organization, the tactics of the employers, the part played by radicals, the attitude of the public, and the outbreak of violence play in the failure of the strike?

4 In 1937 the Congress of Industrial Organizations (C.I.O.) successfully organized the steel industry. If you had been a C.I.O. leader responsible for the organizing drive, what lessons would you have drawn from the 1919 strike?

I

THE STEELWORKERS' DEMANDS

On July 20, 1919, the National Committee for Organizing Iron and Steel Workers formulated the following demands. ☐ From *The Great Steel Strike and Its Lessons*, by William Z. Foster, p. 77. Copyright © 1920 by B. W. Huebsch, Inc. Reprinted by permission of The Viking Press, Inc.

1. Right of collective bargaining
2. Reinstatement of all men discharged for union activities with pay for time lost
3. Eight hour day
4. One day's rest in seven
5. Abolition of 24-hour shift
6. Increases in wages sufficient to guarantee American standard of living
7. Standard scales of wages in all trades and classifications of workers
8. Double rates of pay for all overtime after 8 hours, holiday and Sunday work
9. Check-off system of collecting union dues and assessments
10. Principles of seniority to apply in the maintenance, reduction and increase of working forces
11. Abolition of company unions
12. Abolition of physical examination of applicants for employment

The attitude of the United States Steel Corporation is indicated in the following excerpts from a letter written to the National Committee by Elbert H. Gary on August 27. Gary was the chief executive officer of the company. ☐ *The Great Steel Strike and Its Lessons,* pp. 80–81.

We do not think you are authorized to represent the sentiment of a majority of the employees of the United States Steel Corporation . . . .

As heretofore publicly stated and repeated, our Corporation and subsidiaries, although they do not combat labor unions as such, decline to discuss business with them. The Corporation and subsidiaries are opposed to the "closed shop." They stand for the "open shop," which permits one to engage in any line of employment whether one does or does not belong to a labor union. . . .

In all decisions and acts of the Corporation and subsidiaries pertaining to employees and employment their interests are of highest importance. In wage rates, living and working conditions, conservation of life and health, care and comfort in times of sickness or old age, and providing facilities for the general welfare and happiness of employees and their families, the Corporation and subsidiaries have endeavored to occupy a leading and advanced position among employers.

It will be the object of the Corporation and subsidiaries to give such consideration to employees as to show them their loyal and efficient service in the past is appreciated, and that they may expect in the future fair treatment.

II

THE STRIKE CALL

Union attempts to negotiate with employers failed. William Z. Foster, a militant leader of the National Committee, decided against further delay. Despite a plea from President Wilson and efforts of Samuel Gompers to continue discussions, the following call for a national work stoppage on September 22 was issued. Approximately 340,000 steelworkers walked out. □ From *The Great Steel Strike and Its Lessons,* by William Z. Foster, pp. 94–95. Copyright © 1920 by B. W. Huebsch, Inc. Reprinted by permission of The Viking Press, Inc.

The workers in the iron and steel mills and blast furnaces, not working under union agreements, are requested not to go to work on September 22, and to refuse to resume their employment until such time as the demands of the organizations have been conceded by the steel corporations.

The union committees have tried to arrange conferences with the heads of the steel companies in order that they might present our legitimate demands for the right of collective bargaining, higher wages, shorter hours and better working conditions. But the employers have steadfastly refused to meet them. . . . [In] our stoppage of work let there be no violence. The American Federation of Labor has won all its great progress by peaceful and legal methods.

IRON AND STEEL WORKERS! A historic decision confronts us. If we will but stand together now like men our demands will soon be granted and a golden era of prosperity will open for us in the steel industry. But if we falter and fail to act this great effort will be lost, and we will sink back into a miserable and hopeless serfdom. The welfare of our wives and children is at stake. Now is the time to insist upon our rights as human beings.

STOP WORK SEPTEMBER 22

NATIONAL COMMITTEE
FOR ORGANIZING IRON AND STEEL WORKERS.

III

ERUPTION OF VIOLENCE

Disorder and violence, including rioting, broke out in many sections of the nation which were affected by the strike. The following selection is an excerpt from a news article describing the situation in the great steel area of Pittsburgh. □ "Troopers Stop Meetings," *The New York Times*, September 22, 1919, p. 1. Copyright © 1919 by The New York Times Company. Reprinted by permission.

PITTSBURGH, Sept. 21.—Clashes between Pennsylvania State police and crowds bent on holding labor mass meetings in the Pittsburgh district today ushered in the strike in the iron and steel industry. The most serious disturbance occurred at North Clairton, twenty miles from Pittsburgh, late in the afternoon, where the State troopers charged a crowd of union men holding a mass meeting and broke it up. Resistance was offered, and it is charged by union leaders that the mounted policemen used their clubs vigorously and injured a number in the crowd. . . .

According to eyewitnesses the meeting was proceeding quietly when the State police appeared. The crowd scattered, and some ran up a railroad embankment and threw stones and other missiles at the troopers. During the mêlée several in the crowd were struck on the head by the policemen, it was said. . . . William Z. Foster, Secretary of the National Committee for Organizing Iron and Steel Workers, tonight said that a vigorous protest would be lodged with the State Government against what he termed a "murderous attack upon law-abiding people."

As the strike gained momentum in Gary, Indiana, state militia had difficulty maintaining order. The mayor of Gary appealed to the governor of Indiana, who in turn called for federal troops. Major General Leonard A. Wood and 1000 U.S. soldiers were dispatched to Gary. □ "Gen. Wood Takes Command in Gary," *The New York Times,* October 7, 1919, p. 1. Copyright © 1919 by The New York Times Company. Reprinted by permission.

General Wood, following a two-hour conference with the Gary authorities and strike leaders, issued a proclamation at 10:45 o'clock placing the city under martial law. His first act was to forbid ex-soldiers among the strikers to wear the uniform of the army. . . .

No disturbances occurred during the early part of the day, but at noon pickets began pouring out into the streets by hundreds. As a taunt to the four companies of Indiana reserve militia, scarcely 300 strong, several hundred ex-soldiers among the strikers donned their uniforms and walked the streets displaying pickets badges.

The strikers were distinguishable from the soldiers only by the rifles which the latter carried. The pickets, in some portions of the city, attempted to organize in a semblance of military formation and in some instances attempts were made to pick fights with the soldiers on duty.

When the crowds began to openly jeer and hoot the militia Mayor Hodges hurriedly outlined the situation to Governor Goodrich by telephone and the Governor called for the Federal troops. . . .

Thousands of men lined the sidewalks and hooted at the troops as they marched by, yelling, "Who won the war?" and "Run the tin soldiers home," but there was little disorder, only seven men being arrested during the day.

Both the mill officials and General Wood agreed that sending of federal troops was a wise move. □ "Gen. Wood's Men Restore Order in Gary Strike Zone," *The New York Times,* October 8, 1919, p. 1. Copyright © 1919 by the New York Times Company. Reprinted by permission.

The mill officials [in Gary] are pleased that the regulars have been called in, for men who had been holding back for fear of violence, they said, would now rush back to work. The strikers were pleased, too, they said, for they were now assured of a square deal. . . .

"It was evident," the General said, "that the city officials of Gary were extremely nervous. The strikers, nearly all of whom are aliens, and a good many of whom cannot speak English, paraded the streets in defiance of the municipality, and declared their determination to continue the street demonstrations. The police were unable to stop them. The worst influence came from certain Red agitators, whose only desire seemingly was to foment trouble. The best labor element stands absolutely for law and order."

The following is a report from a union official who recorded the testimony of John Simpel, a worker at the Carnegie Steel Company in Newcastle, Pennsylvania. □ From *The Great Steel Strike and Its Lessons,* by William Z. Foster, p. 128. Copyright © 1920 by B. W. Huebsch, Inc. Reprinted by permission of the Viking Press, Inc.

John Simpel, 1711 Morris Ave., Newcastle.

On Sept. 22, about 5:30 P.M. he was walking along towards his home on Moravia Street. Hearing shots fired he stopped in the middle of the street and was instantly struck by bullets three times, one bullet going through his leg, one through his finger, while the third entered his back and went through his body, coming out through his abdomen. The shots were fired from inside the gates of the Carnegie Steel Company's plant. Mr. Simpel believes the shots were fired from a machine gun, because of their rapid succession. He fell on the ground and lay there for about ten minutes, until he was picked up by a young boy. . . . He is now totally disabled. He has a wife and a child and is 48 years of age. . . .

JAS. A. NORRINGTON, Secretary.

IV

APPEALS TO PREJUDICE

Opponents of the strike at the National Tube Company plant in Elwood, Pennsylvania, appealed to prejudice against foreign-born workers in order to create suspicion and disunity. The handbill which follows was circulated to incite native Americans against Italian workmen. □ From *The Great Steel Strike and Its Lessons,* by William Z. Foster, p. 199. Copyright © 1920 by B. W. Huebsch, Inc. Reprinted by permission of The Viking Press, Inc.

WAKE UP AMERICANS!!

ITALIAN LABORERS, organized under the American Federation of Labor are going to strike Monday and are threatening workmen who want to continue working.

These foreigners have been told by labor agitators that if they would join the union they would get Americans' jobs.

They are being encouraged by ITALIAN MERCHANTS, who are in sympathy with them.

ARE YOU GOING TO SLEEP AND LET MOB RULE THREATEN THE PEACE OF OUR TOWN?

A South Carolina Negro, recruited to work during the stoppage, tells his story. □ *The Great Steel Strike and Its Lessons,* pp. 207–208.

I arrived in Monessen on Wednesday, November 19. There were about 200 of us loaded in the cars at Baltimore; some were white; and when we were loaded in the cars were told that we were being taken to Philadelphia.

We were not told that a strike was in progress. . . .

When we took the train a guard locked the doors so that we were unable to get out, and no meals were given us on the way, although we were promised board.

We were unloaded at Lock 4 and had a guard placed over us, and were then marched into the grounds of the Pittsburgh Steel Products Co. We were then told to go to work, and when I found out that there was a strike on I got out. They refused to let me out at the gate when I protested about working, and I climbed over the fence and they caught me and compelled me to go back and sign a paper and told me that I would have to go to work. I told them that I would not go to work if they kept me there two years. I was placed on a boat. There were about 200 other people there. The guards informed me that if I made any attempt to again run away that they would shoot me. I got a rope and escaped, as I will not work to break the strike.

Racial violence flared as Negroes crossed picket lines. Use of strikebreakers was considered an important factor in the failure of the strike. ☐ "Negroes Open Fire on Donora Strikers," *The New York Times,* October 10, 1919, p. 4. Copyright ©️ 1919 by The New York Times Company. Reprinted by permission.

PITTSBURGH, Oct. 9.—Two men were shot and several were hit with bricks in a riot at Donora this morning when a number of negroes, returning to work at the plant of the American Steel and Wire Company, opened fire with revolvers in return for an attack with missiles by strikers.

Both of the wounded men are foreigners, who can not speak English. One was shot in the right ankle and the other in the knee. Several more negro laborers were hurt. State police arrived immediately after the shooting and scattered the crowd.

V

REFUSAL TO WALK OUT

At a critical point in the strike, certain unions with working contracts failed to support the National Committee's call for an industry-wide strike. The following excerpt indicates the position of one such organization. ☐ "Amalgamated Acts to Start Up Plants," *The New York Times,* October 10, 1919, p. 4. Copyright © by The New York Times Company. Reprinted by permission.

PITTSBURGH, Oct. 9.—Strike leaders were greatly interested today in the efforts of the Amalgamated Association of Iron, Steel and Tin Workers to settle the strike in plants where the association has agreements. In some mills where the association has agreements men walked out, causing the places to shut down and throwing amalgamated men out of work.

"The Amalgamated Association," said D. J. Davis, Assistant International President of that organization today, "must uphold its contracts with the steel companies. We do not intend to let the steel strike interfere with these agreements.

"The Amalgamated will attempt to negotiate working agreements for the men employed in these industries although they are not members of the association." . . . Where Amalgamated men voluntarily went on strike, Mr. Davis said, they did so through a misunderstanding of orders.

Efforts are being made to open independent plants in the Pittsburgh District having Amalgamated agreements, but closed by the strike of other steel workers, Mr. Davis said.

Continuation of work in the large plants of the Bethlehem Steel Corporation was an important reason for the ultimate failure of the strike. ☐ "Bethlehem is Apathetic," *The New York Times,* September 30, 1919, p. 1. Copyright © 1919 by The New York Times Company. Reprinted by permission.

BETHLEHEM, Penn., Sept. 29.—With the strike in the plants of the Bethlehem Steel Corporation here and at Lebanon, Reading, Steelton, and Sparrows Point less than eighteen hours old, it appears tonight that the strikers have lost already. Unless they are able to execute some powerful strategic move very quickly a speedy and permanent victory for the company seems inevitable.

Reports from the mills outside Bethlehem indicate that the walkout had little or no effect upon operations, while here, where the leaders' efforts were fairly well concentrated, actual observation of conditions points to their having fallen far short of their objective, a paralysis of the corporation's great plants. . . .

Thus far it has been a remarkable strike. There has been practically no disorder. The day's total of arrests is four. There has not been a sign of riot. This very absence of the turmoil, and clubbing, and shooting, and mob-driving which has marked so many struggles of this sort may prove a large factor in defeating the strikers, for no one at all familiar with conditions here, whether he be workman or boss, citizen or neutral observer, denies that many of those who stayed away today did so because they were intimidated or terrorized by their own fears. The company confidently expects that if the early morning hours are as peaceful as today has been this class of men will return to their posts.

VI

ATTITUDE OF THE PUBLIC PRESS

A great majority of newspapers in 1919 supported the position of the steel corporations in upholding the open shop and opposing general strikes. The following excerpt from a *New York Times* editorial reflects the pro-business attitude of the American press.   ☐ "The Dying Steel Strike," *The New York Times,* September 30, 1919, p. 18. Copyright © 1919 by The New York Times Company. Reprinted by permission.

With the Bethlehem fizzle the initiative passes from the strikers to the employers. The attack has failed, and the attackers are now on the defense. That their condition worries them is shown by their efforts to induce the four railway brotherhoods to reconsider the refusal by one of them to take sympathetic action. Next to the railway brotherhoods the steel strikers are the best paid class of labor in the country. The spectacle of these two classes acting sympathetically against other workers and the entire country would be one of more danger to them than to the country, for the echo would be louder than the original protest against the steel strike. Labor agitation met its Waterloo when President Wilson declared that the vicious circle of increases of wages and the cost of living must be broken. It is in vain that the steel strikers are looking for some Blücher [a Prussian general who helped defeat Napoleon], from Bethlehem or elsewhere, to rescue them from their dilemma. A defeat . . . would be the public's best protection against an endless series of annoyances, but none with less justification than the steel strike.

VII

REACTION AGAINST THE REDS

Fear of communism helped rally public sentiment against the steel strike. Agitation among the strikers by the newly established Communist Party of America helped to feed the fear.   ☐ "Reds Call Gary Strikers to Rise and Oust Troops," *The New York Times,* October 14, 1919, p. 1. Copyright © 1919 by The New York Times Company. Reprinted by permission.

CHICAGO, Oct. 13.—Purporting to be a proclamation of the Communist Party of America, a hand bill advocating overthrow of the military in Gary was given to correspondents at the afternoon conference with Colonel

W. H. Mapes, commander of the troops. He said that four copies were found on a striker who was stopped on the street by Secret Service men, but not arrested.

"This is the most dangerous piece of literature that has ever come to my attention," said Colonel Mapes. "Other Red pamphlets have been severe but the subject matter has been usually general in direction. This is a direct appeal to the followers to overthrow the Federal troops in Gary. It is a most dangerous situation to deal with and it will be dealt with accordingly.

"Before we leave we intend to clean Gary of Red agitators."

Colonel Mapes has caused all printing shops in the district to be visited in an effort to ascertain where the proclamation was printed. The document reads:

"THE CAPITALISTS CHALLENGE YOU WORKINGMEN.
"PROCLAMATION OF
THE COMMUNIST PARTY OF AMERICA.

"Martial law has been declared in Gary, Ind. Soldiers of the regular army, soldiers who have seen service overseas, who have waded through the blood of their fellows on the battlefields of Europe, as the capitalist press is gloatingly declaring, are now in control.

"The army of occupation entered Gary fully equipped. Automatic rifles, rifles, hand grenades, machine guns and heavier cannon, cannon that can clear two miles of a city street in a few minutes, as the officer in charge said. These are ready for use in Gary, and the soldiers wear trench helmets made by the workers of Gary. . . .

"The workingmen of Gary are engaged in a struggle against the capitalists. They have suffered long. Low wages, long hours of exhausting work in the heat of the steel ovens, life sapping toil with no time for home life, this has been their lot.

"At last they revolted. Risking suffering and hunger, risking the assault of the brutal bullies of the steel trust, who do not stop even at murder, they resorted to the strike to make their masters lighten the conditions of their toil. They organized their power and united dared challenge to a test of strength the industrial octopus which dominated the steel industry.

"Gary is the city of steel. It was built by the order of the Steel Trust. The influence and control of the Steel Trust extends to every nook and corner of the life of the city. Its spies are everywhere. The local government is its tool and expresses its will. This Steel Trust municipal government forbade the workingmen to show their solidarity by parades and by public meetings.

"It hoped by keeping the workers apart to break their spirit, to give encouragement to the few scabs who were working."

VIII

COLLAPSE OF THE STEEL STRIKE

In January 1920, the National Committee released the following telegram presenting its analysis of the reasons for failure of the strike. ☐ From *The Great Steel Strike and Its Lessons*, by William Z. Foster, pp. 192–193. Copyright © 1920 by B. W. Huebsch, Inc. Reprinted by permission of The Viking Press, Inc.

The Steel Corporations, with the active assistance of the press, the courts, the federal troops, state police, and many public officials, have denied steel workers their rights of free speech, free assembly and the right to organize, and by this arbitrary and ruthless misuse of power have brought about a condition which has compelled the National Committee for Organizing Iron and Steel Workers to vote today that the active strike phase of the steel campaign is now at an end. A vigorous campaign of education and re-organization will be immediately begun and will not cease until industrial justice has been achieved in the steel industry. All steel strikers are now at liberty to return to work pending preparations for the next big organization movement.

PROBLEM 10

Welfare Capitalism

From 1920 to 1933 the membership of American trade unions declined steadily from 5,110,000 to 2,500,000. The outbreak of the depression in 1930 accelerated the decline because many organized workers became unemployed and could not pay dues. The drop in membership that occurred during the prosperous years 1920-1929, however, grew out of a different set of causes.

Since the Civil War the membership of trade unions had increased consistently during periods of prosperity. Full production meant high employment. Under these conditions the employer was less likely to resist demands for either union recognition or the adjustment of grievances. But during the boom years of the 1920's, unions declined. A peculiar combination of circumstances accounts for this unusual development.

The decline of union membership in basic industry resulted in part from the loss of the friendly Wilson administration. The three Republican administrations of the 1920's were all closely allied to business. Moreover, vastly improved methods of production increased industrial output without a significant increase in the national labor force. Factory wages rose slowly but steadily despite the decline of the unions. In addition, the A.F. of L. leadership refused to support industrial unions throughout the 1920's, and the old-line craft structure was unsuited to the needs of mass production industry.

At least equal in importance to any of these factors was the introduction by management of new personnel policies. Many concerns adopted plans of profit sharing, stock distribution, vacation and retirement funds, group life insurance, medical care, recreational activities, company-financed housing, and security from unemployment. As a direct alternative to trade unions, a host of firms established employee representation associations (company unions) or provided labor representation on various committees.

This new concern on the part of business for its employees was termed "welfare capitalism." Some Americans hailed it as the advent of a new era of industrial harmony. Others criticized it as a form of benevolent despotism. Neither attitude could change the fact that a contented employee could be as great an obstacle to union organization as an obstinate employer.

The readings which follow include examples of welfare capitalism in operation and some comments from friends and critics of the new order. As you read, think of the following questions:

1 What advantages to employers are indicated by George Eastman in his description of welfare capitalism? Why is he proud of the comment characterizing his program as one of "damned intelligent self-interest"?

2 Is Eastman's concern for the welfare of aging employees, as expressed in his letter of July 19, 1929, the main reason that the company adopted the pension plan? Should Eastman be judged by his motives or by the results achieved for his employees? Explain.

3 Why did Philip Wagner object to the company union? Would most union members share his point of view? Explain.

4 After the economic crash of 1929, many corporations abandoned their welfare programs. What evidence (if any) do you see in these readings to indicate why a depression would undermine them?

5 In what way might welfare capitalism have contributed to the decrease of union membership during the 1920's?

I

A PIONEER OF WELFARE CAPITALISM

George Eastman was the founder of the Eastman Kodak Company, a prime example of a firm that has successfully utilized welfare capitalism. This statement by Eastman was included in a booklet distributed to Kodak employees in December 1927 when a new retirement plan was announced. □ Used by permission of Eastman Kodak Company.

It is with a great deal of satisfaction, to me and to the Management, that we announce a retirement annuity plan, together with a life insurance and disability benefit plan for Kodak employees.

Broadly, the purpose is to provide not merely a substantial annuity for old age—this annuity to be paid by a financially solid insurance company—but also a substantial protection in the form of life insurance and liberal treatment under the disability plan. . . .

To put this plan into immediate effect requires a very large investment for the liabilities which have already accrued, covering the past services of employees. It is proposed that this payment, which will total approximately six and one-half million dollars, be made one-half by funds appropriated by the Company and one-half by the Kodak Employees Association.

The funds of the Kodak Employees Association, it will be recalled, were originally contributed by the Company and myself for the welfare of the employees. . . . The Kodak Employees Association fund is, however, inadequate for the purpose; accordingly the Management feels that this plan, which will provide liberally for retirement annuities, life insurance, and disability benefits, should be established. The plan has been approved by the members and directors of the Kodak Employees Association. . . .

This plan will not interfere with the assistance which the Kodak Employees Association has heretofore given employees in financing their homes through second mortgages, as the Kodak Company will assume the responsibility of providing the Association with sufficient funds for carrying on this meritorious work.

The Company and the Kodak Employees Association having thus provided for the initial financing, it is necessary that the present rate of the wage dividend be reduced in order to provide funds for the future payments to be made to the insurance company.

When the wage dividend was established, the purpose, first of all, was that it should provide employees, in a lump sum annually, with a sufficient amount of money for investment so that, after a reasonable period of service, the employee would have accumulated from these wage dividends sufficient property to produce an income during old age. Of course, it was also the intention that employees who contribute so largely to the success of the Company should, through the wage dividend, share in the profits coming from its success; yet of even greater importance in the minds of the directors was the idea that these wage dividends would enable the employees . . . to provide against disability and . . . old age. . . .

. . . With the wage dividend, which gives the employee a share in the profits of the Company; the sickness benefit plan, which provides a liberal allowance in case of illness; this retirement annuity, life insurance, and disability benefit plan; and with the facilities offered the employees by the Kodak Employees Association for financing their homes, and the facilities offered the employees by the Eastman Savings and Loan Association for investing their savings—I feel that a comprehensive program of industrial relations has now been established. I congratulate the employees upon the work that has been accomplished.

II

EVOLUTION OF THE EASTMAN PLAN

The comprehensive welfare program of the Eastman Kodak Company developed gradually over many years. These excerpts from letters written by George Eastman to friends and business associates help to explain the evolution of the system and the attitude of the company toward it. □ Used by permission of Eastman Kodak Company.

MARCH 6, 1912:

My idea in setting these large amounts aside for the welfare fund is that the time may come when our earnings will decrease. At the same time our employees are growing older and unless we make provision now for taking care of needy cases it may be too much of a burden later on. We have not devised any cut and dried plan for disbursing the income from this fund and it is not likely that we will as our experience shows that each case has to be treated on its merits. We have done this heretofore and charged the cost up to operating expenses. Since last April we have been charging such payments to the income from the fund. . . .

. . . [As] far as we have heard from the shareholders there has been not one single objection. The best compliment that I have heard for it is that it was "prompted by damned intelligent self-interest."

APRIL 4, 1919:

The success of the Wage Dividend encourages us to think that this will be actually a money making operation for the company. . . . We have had no strikes and our labor turnover has been less than in any other concern here in Rochester . . . . The Wage Dividend will of course be continued but it does not go quite far enough because it does not give the employees a real proprietary interest in the company. I feel as labor conditions grow more difficult that it will be greatly to the advantage of the company to be a leader, not a follower. One of the great advantages of bringing this to a head now is that it is not done under force of any circumstances. Our employees are well satisfied and loyal and this can only act to make them more so. We are running a very complicated and difficult business. I do not know any that depends more upon the good feeling and faithfulness of its employees.

FEBRUARY 8, 1921:

Up to only about a year ago it had been the custom of the company to treat every case of need not according to a set rule but according to its peculiar necessities and in some instances where employees were sick we not only paid their full salaries but paid them additional money (amounting sometimes to double their salary) to pay for special treatment necessary to promote recovery. This way of treating such matters is in my judgment the most effective way of distributing relief but unfortunately it antagonizes the other employees. There are two objects to be attained in so called welfare work: One is to treat the particular case adequately and the other is to produce a favorable psychological effect upon the other employees. What is done for one sick man creates an impression upon possibly two hundred or five hundred well men. What happened under the old plan was that the employees who were thrifty and had saved money so that they could take care of themselves complained that the company would not do as much for them when they were sick as for some shiftless or improvident co-worker and that therefore our plan really discouraged men from trying to save anything. This view became so general that we finally had to abandon our old plan and adopt a new one. The new plan applies alike to all employees and provides for all the help that it is reasonable to expect any big institution to give its sick and disabled and is more liberal than any plan that we know of that is in use by any large concern. It is certainly more liberal than the average.

JULY 19, 1929:

I have read your paper on age efficiency with a good deal of interest. There is a good deal in what you say about finding work for the people who retain their efficiency beyond the allotted age. In our own organization, after eighteen years of experiment with wage dividends, which have been paid to our employees without any strings tied to them, we finally concluded to shift to a pension plan which will permit us to lay off men and women who have slackened in their usefulness to the organization. My theory is that we have got to keep up the efficiency of our organization in preference to any other considerations because unless the Company can earn money it cannot confer benefits beyond ordinary wages.

III

PROFIT SHARING AMONG SOAP WORKERS

This selection, describing the profit-sharing plan of a large soap manufacturer, was written by Herbert Feis, who, at the time, was a professor of economics. □ Herbert Feis, "Workers as Capitalists," *The American Review of Reviews*, Vol. 77, April 1928, pp. 400, 401, 402, 403–404.

The old basis of American democracy and equality has vanished, and vanished permanently. In the past the poorest immigrant coming to the United States could hope to acquire some part of our fields, forests and pastures; and the resulting widespread ownership of land provided a solid foundation of economic fact for democracy. But now more than three-quarters of our people are cut off from the land. They live in small homes in our cities and towns, herded together near the factories that have replaced farms as the scene of America's major work. Thus the old basis of equality has disappeared.

Is there a new one to be found? Or do we face the perspective drawn by nineteenth century European experience—on top a small number of the colossally rich in highly concentrated control of industry, and at the bottom great numbers of workers living on uncertain earnings, possessing little or nothing, incapable of rising—an industrial proletariat?

The future of the United States seems to lie largely in the answer to this question. Hence the interest and encouragement bestowed upon all signs that wage-earners are acquiring a share in the ownership of industrial property by purchase of corporate securities. In that tendency many see the origin of a new form of economic democracy. They see in it also the strongest protection against those most pressing needs and dangers which in Europe have led to social insurance systems. Many employers hope that from the spread of employee ownership of corporate securities there will result closer coöperation between management and men, the end of industrial strife, and the wiping out of notions of class conflict. . . .

The plan for the encouragement of stock ownership (the Profit-Sharing Plan) of the Procter and Gamble Company has a longer continuous history than that of almost any similar arrangement—having been framed in 1886. Both in the manager's offices and in the workshops its place in the company's scheme of existence is beyond question. The company, it will be recalled, makes soaps, glycerine, glycerine products, and food products manufactured from cottonseed oil and cocoanut oil. . . .

The essentials of the plan are simple. Its direct objects have been two: first, to aid and encourage saving by employees; secondly, to build up a sense of common interest between management and men. . . .

All workers whose wages are below $2,000 a year may participate after six months of employment. . . .

Thus a factory hand who joins the company in June at a wage of $30 a week may apply, in December, for stock worth $1,560—eight shares, say, if the stock should be selling for $195 in the market. The company advances the money to buy this stock; and it applies toward its purchase by the employee $156 a year to begin with, and more as his length of service grows. Meanwhile the employee himself pays $1.50 from his salary each week toward purchase of the stock. In six years it would be paid for. He would then own the eight shares, and receive regular dividends on them, although he had contributed less than one-third the cost from his wages.

Any profit-sharer is free to quit the plan at any time, and for any reasons. If he drops out before he has been in the plan a year, he receives back merely what he has paid in out of his wages; if his length of membership exceeds a year, he receives such stock as is fully paid up. Furthermore, the company guarantees that if, at the termination of the worker's employment for any reason whatsoever, the market value of the stock he has acquired is less than its original cost, this original cost will be refunded. . . .

The encouragement to stock accumulation within the company has thus been strong. The risk of loss has been virtually absent, and, because of the company's prolonged record of prosperity and constant rise in the market value of its stock, the chances of large gain have been good. Wages compare well with those in the locality. . . .

I began this article with a reference to the promise of a profound economic influence which many see in the present workings of the employee stock-ownership plan. My investigation into the experience of this one company indicates that the plan is well established and regarded as a distinct advantage of being in the employment of the company. . . . It has helped many men to accumulate much needed holdings, men who otherwise probably would not have a cent.

The industrial workers will own part of the properties which employ them for the first time since the Industrial Revolution; but that ownership is likely to be only a minor fraction, widely distributed. Some, the more able, steady, and saving, will be definitely in the small property class. And if the present surge of American industry continues, other plans for employee stock acquisition may outrun the Procter and Gamble plan, although there are too many elements of uncertainty to permit precise prediction.

IV

A CRITIC OF WELFARE CAPITALISM

Philip Wagner, in the following reading, refers to welfare capitalism as the "New Industrial Humanism." Concentrating on company unions, plant publications sponsored by management, and other "fringe benefits," Wagner illustrates the skeptical attitude of many workers. □ Philip Wagner, "The New Humanism in Industry," *American Mercury,* Vol. 21, October 1930, pp. 175, 176, 177, 178, 180–181, 182, 183.

The name of the prophet who first proclaimed the New Industrial Humanism has somehow been lost; but his spirit, like that of the unknown soldier, marches on. The body of doctrine that he fathered . . . got its first real workout in a few factories while the war was on, but a full-fledged movement did not develop from it until the doughboys had come home. . . .

The idea itself was simple: Why not start treating these workmen like men and brothers? . . . A smoke screen of Humanism would at least obscure the sharp lines of the labor battle; and once the formation is destroyed, labor breaks down into the individuals who compose it, much pleasanter to deal with, much easier to pull around by the nose.

The technique developed for doing this was pleasantly simple and very much like the working formula of the politician. It consisted of two elements: the boloney element, and that of practical concession.

The boloney was introduced into industrial relations through several channels, but the most successful was the company union. . . . When it was first talked of the company union was naturally looked on with some suspicion by the older industrialists, but presently, after its power to quiet the grunts of organized labor had been demonstrated by the war-time pioneers, there was a rush to adopt it. . . .

So between 1918 and 1927 the number of plants adopting some form of company unionism trebled, and the number of employés working in these plants reached two millions. . . .

The chief purpose of the company union is to keep out the regular union, or else let it out by the back door if it is already established. . . .

The first sign that a factory is about to be treated to a company union is an unaccustomed interest among the foremen and the more exalted bosses in Industrial Democracy. Superintendents begin to talk loftily at annual banquets about "giving the worker a voice" and "providing channels of expression." These words gradually get the ears of the workmen, producing in them a vague and somewhat incredulous curiosity. After the ground has been thus prepared, a plan for "bringing the elected representatives of the workmen into the councils of the management" is suddenly trotted out. Printed copies of a constitution are distributed; a campaign of persuasion is begun. . . .

The representatives are chosen amid a great clatter of ballot-boxes. Thereafter they meet at regular intervals on company time (a necessary detail) and transact their business, such as it is. . . .

In almost every case the meeting is a one-ring circus, with the superintendent or the works manager doing the performing. In these Humanistic days a boss is no longer a sour-faced driver. A new type has sprung up to take the place of the old-fashioned tyrant. The typical superintendent of today must combine other qualities with the traditional gifts of the administrator. He must have a ready smile, preferably with a tooth or two missing (to look more democratic). . . . He must be quick at response and an adept in the arts of flattery; he should also possess a Dominant Personality. He must, in short, be of the kind who are always the Life of the Party and Masters of the Situation; for it devolves upon him to keep the parliamentary mummery going, and going briskly, for at least an hour twice a month.

The first hitch in the conduct of one of these meetings comes when the minutes of the previous meeting have been read.

"And now, gentlemen," smiles the superintendent from the chair, "is there any new business?"

There is a long pause. Then he continues.

"Are there any reports from committees? Perhaps the Health and Hazards Committee has something to say?" He turns to the chairman of the Health and Hazards Committee, whose first name he has been careful to remember. "What do you say, Jimmie? Got any report to make?"

Jimmie can never get used to having the superintendent call him by his first name. It affects him violently. It upsets all of his old labor union convictions about robber barons and exploiters of the poor. He gets to his feet. "Well," he says, twisting his machinist's cap in his hands and trying hard to think up a grievance, "all I got to say is that we hadda couple kicks about the toilet down in Building 46-C. She ain't been flushin', as you might say, quite right."

"Fine, Jimmie!" cries the superintendent. "That's what I want all of you boys to do. Just speak right up. The only way we fellows can get together on these problems is to lay our cards right down on the table. Nothing clears the air like a little frank discussion, boys." . . .

Another important cog in the boloney-making machinery is the plant magazine. This new species of journal, like the company union, is a war baby.

Fifteen years ago it was almost unheard of. Now no self-respecting manufacturing plant is without its own organ of opinion. The latest census, conducted by *Printers' Ink,* includes the names of approximately 800 of them, and their combined circulation runs into the millions. . . .

Unfortunately the use of boloney, whether in company union meetings or in plant magazines, has its limits. . . . Certain employers have learned to their acute distress that the most gullible group of workmen in the world will presently cease to be gulled if they get nothing tangible. . . .

The notions of employers as to what constitutes such a gesture vary considerably. There is Mr. Schwab's [Charles M. Schwab, a steel magnate] celebrated dictum about the need for cultivating musical sensibility among steel workers. . . .

Dr. L. Grace Powell Sitzer, who humanizes the girls employed by Wrigley, the gum man, has other notions. Her idea of a tangible gesture is to give her girls hot food for lunch, at cost; for, as she says, "girls who eat hot food at noon produce more work in the afternoon than those who carry a cold lunch from home." Dr. Sitzer has also introduced other tangible gestures. She is credited, for instance, with the scheme of giving every female employé a free shampoo once a month, on company time. . . .

Eastman Kodak, Hershey Chocolate, the LeBlond Machine Tool Company of Cincinnati and many others have found that the efforts of landscape gardeners and horticulturalists afford much spiritual comfort to their workers, and have planned and maintained elaborate park systems. . . .

G. A. Pennock, of the Western Electric Company, whose papers on restroom installation and maintenance are classics and have given him the title to speak with authority, feels that adequate, not to say sumptuous, rest-rooms are a worthwhile investment. . . .

With characteristic efficiency the industrialists have organized and standardized their distribution of favors. All forward-looking factories now have their Industrial Relations Departments, each of which is a sort of permanent check on the conscience of the management. These Industrial Relations Departments organize sporting competitions. . . . They promote minstrel shows. They manage, in most plants, to arrange for an annual Family Day, which gives all the kiddies a chance to see where daddy works, and, with lollypop juice (from free and contented lollypops) dripping from the corners of their mouths, to take a ride on the overhead crane or the bed of the planing mill. They also promote noon-hour dances and band concerts and movie shows. . . .

The plums which enlightened employers now hand out are not limited, either, to those in the custody of the industrial relations boys. There are a great many which affect the employé's pocketbook directly and which are doled out of the management's bag one at a time and with as long an interval between as discretion dictates. . . .

The varieties of bonus or incentive plans are so many, however, that it is quite impossible to catalogue them all. Almost every plant has one, if only the practice of handing out gifts of cash at Christmas time; and all of them are alike in that the management greatly prefers them to granting raises in pay. A bonus, after all, is a bonus. It is a treat. It need not necessarily be repeated. It does not come back to plague the boss with his generosity every week, the way a raise does.

Another widely adopted scheme is that of giving away free insurance to employés who have served a specified length of time. This helps to reduce employment turnover and saves the company a good deal in burial costs. . . .

A number of concerns are, with certain misgivings, yielding to the growing demand for adequate old-age pensions in which both employés and employers participate. . . . Still another variation is the plan of guaranteeing a second mortgage for an employé. This makes it easier to buy a home with a small down payment, and incidentally ties the happy victim still closer to the company. . . .

It pays. That is the key to the popularity of the New Industrial Humanism. And for proof one has only to examine the history of organized labor and industrial bargaining during the past decade. Certain of the unions are still powerful; but in most cases they are in the trades which do not as a rule deal day after day with large manufacturers. In the big manufacturing industries organized labor has not only failed to make advances; it has fallen back. And in certain of the newer industries, notably automobile manufacturing, the unions haven't even squeezed a wedge in.

The American Federation has lost in prestige and in numbers. Once militant, it is now conciliatory; and its organ, the *Federationist,* spends endless space discussing "coöperation" and the "mutual interests" of employer and employé. The Hon. William Green, president of this once-militant engine of the labor cause, is now much in demand as an after-dinner speaker at conventions of manufacturers, where he and the erstwhile enemies of labor sit around all evening and spray perfume on one another. . . .

The workers are kept so busy being grateful that they have little time for grousing. Now and then, perhaps, a few get the notion that all isn't quite so well as it might be. But that notion is vague, and presently another outing comes along and the faint spark of discontent is smothered under a thick blanket of fried fish, potato salad and ice cream.

PROBLEM 11

A New Deal for Labor

The Great Crash of 1929 plunged the economy into depression and undermined the stability of labor relations which welfare capitalism had helped to achieve. Consequently, the government was drawn into efforts to revive economic activity and to restore labor peace simultaneously.

As early as 1932 the Norris-LaGuardia Act had prohibited companies from discharging employees for union activity and had shielded unions against court injunctions. With the inauguration in 1933 of Franklin D. Roosevelt's New Deal administration, the federal government undertook comprehensive legislation known as the National Industrial Recovery Act to reorganize the whole structure of American industry. As part of a network of codes of fair business practices drafted under this act, workers were to be guaranteed the right to bargain collectively through unions of their choice. Provisions were also included for maximum hours, minimum wages, and suitable working conditions. The attempt to solve all industrial problems in this manner soon bogged down. In 1935 the N.I.R.A. was ruled unconstitutional by the Supreme Court. In the following three years Congress enacted several specific measures, each aimed at a different aspect of the labor problem. The Social Security Act provided unemployment insurance and old-age pensions. The

Works Progress Administration offered relief through federal jobs to the unemployed. The Fair Labor Standards Act prohibited child labor and set minimum wages and maximum hours. The establishment of a National Labor Relations Board promoted collective bargaining through which unions might be certified as the recognized bargaining agent for a particular group of employees. A union might appeal to the Board against certain designated unfair labor practices of an employer to obstruct or prevent collective bargaining.

The readings which follow illustrate the philosophy behind the New Deal measures and indicate how some of them worked in practice. As you read, consider the following questions:

1 Who are the "special groups" referred to by President Roosevelt in the first paragraph of Reading I? In your opinion, would the promoters of welfare capitalism of the 1920's be members of these groups?

2 How did labor regulations of the New Deal change the bargaining situation? Why could unions in the steel industry succeed in this new context where they had failed in 1919?

3 To what did Roosevelt attribute failure of the government to settle industrial disputes? Is he objective in eliminating government as a possible source of trouble?

4 In Reading IV, William H. Spencer lists five "assumptions" underlying the Wagner Act. Evaluate the historical validity of these assumptions in the light of evidence drawn from earlier readings.

I

ROOSEVELT SURVEYS THE N.I.R.A.

On March 5, 1934, one year after his inauguration, President Franklin D. Roosevelt analyzed the purposes, accomplishments, and failures of the National Industrial Recovery Act. In the following excerpts from a speech delivered to representatives of six hundred industries, Roosevelt admitted shortcomings of the National Recovery Administration (NRA) and pointed out the need to correct certain errors. □ *Congressional Record*, 73rd Congress, 2nd Session. Volume 78, Part 4, March 5, 1934, pp. 3676–3677.

It was because the situation in March 1933 was so serious all along the line that remedies had to be applied to every phase of the illness. The objective was, as you know, to apply these remedies in the American way and not to copy those which are being tried in other countries which do not live under the same form of democratic government as ours. I am always a little amused and perhaps at times a little saddened—and I think the American people feel the same way—by those few writers and speakers who proclaim tearfully either that we are now committed to Communism and collectivism or that we have adopted Fascism and a dictatorship. The real truth of the matter is that for a number of years in our country the machinery of democracy had failed to function. Through inertia on the part of leaders and on the part of the people themselves the operations of government had fallen into the hands of special groups, some of them vociferously led by people who undertook to obtain special advantages for special classes and others led by a handful of individuals who believed in their superhuman ability to retain in their own hands the entire business and financial control over the economic and social structure of the Nation. . . .

The National Industrial Recovery Act was drawn with the greatest good of the greatest number in mind. Its aim was to increase the buying power of wage earners and farmers so that industry, labor and the public might benefit through building up the market for farm and factory goods. Employer, wage earner, and consumer groups are all represented on its boards with the Government; all three groups with the Government must have the interests of all the people as their main responsibility.

What we seek is balance in our economic system—balance between agriculture and industry and balance between the wage earner, the employer, and the consumer. We seek also balance that our internal markets be kept rich and large, and that our trade with other Nations be increased on both sides of the ledger. . . .

The very conception of N.R.A. follows the democratic procedure of our Government itself. Its theory of self-regulation follows the American method rather than any of the experiments being tried in other Nations. . . .

And now to be more specific in regard to N. R. A. itself. You have set up representative government in industry. You are carrying it on without violation of the constitutional or the parliamentary system to which the United States has been accustomed. Your industrial groups are composed of two parts —labor and management; and the Government is a participant in this organization in order to carry out this mandate of the law. "To promote organization in industry for the purpose of cooperative action in trade groups and to induce and maintain united action of labor and management under adequate Government sanction and supervision." . . .

One more subject I call to your special attention. The law itself has provided for free choice of their own representatives by employees. Those two words "free choice", mean just what they say. It is obvious that the Government itself not only has the right but also the duty to see, first, that employees may make a choice; and, secondly, that in the making of it they shall be wholly free. I ask that the letter and the spirit of free choice be accorded to its workers by every corporation in the United States.

We have been seeking experience in our first 8 months of code making; for that same reason we have been tolerant of certain misunderstandings even when they resulted in evasions of the spirit if not of the letter of the law. Now we are moving into a period of administration when that which is law must be made certain and the letter and the spirit must be fulfilled. We cannot tolerate actions which are clearly monopolistic, which wink at unfair trade practices, which fail to give to labor free choice of their representatives, or which are otherwise hostile to the public interest.

In a word, we cannot tolerate abuses of economic power—abuses against labor, abuses against employers, or abuses against the consuming public,— whether they persist either with the aid of codes or despite their prohibitions. This does not mean that we can at once make perfect many hundred codes covering the major trades and industries of the Nation, nor that we have arrived at the time for taking stock for correcting manifest errors, for rooting out demonstrated evils.

II

A CODE OF FAIR PRACTICES

Following are excerpts from The Bituminous Coal Code, one of the hundreds of codes of fair competition written under the NRA. Roosevelt characterized these regulations as the fruit of "representative government in industry." □ *The New Deal and Business Recovery,* by W. E. Davies and William Goetzmann, pp. 21–24, copyright © 1960 (Problem 6 of Manning and Potter's *Government and the American Economy: 1870—Present,* copyright © 1950). Reprinted by permission of the publishers, Holt, Rinehart and Winston, Inc.

Article III—Maximum Hours of Labor

No employee, except members of the executive, supervisory, technical, and confidential personnel, shall be employed in excess of 40 hours in any calendar week after the effective date of this Code. No employee shall be required or permitted to work more than eight hours in any one day at usual working places or otherwise in or about the mine (exclusive of lunch period), whether paid by the hour or on a tonnage or other piecework basis. . . .

The foregoing maximum hours of work shall not be construed as a minimum; and if at any mine a majority of the employed workers express their desire, by written request to the employer, to share available work with bona fide unemployed workers of the same mine, the number of hours' work may be adjusted accordingly by mutual agreement between such employed workers and their employees.

Article IV—Minimum Rates of Pay

The basic minimum rate for inside skilled labor and the basic minimum rate for outside common labor shall be the rate hereinafter set forth in Schedule "A" for each district therein described. . . .

[Examples of minimum rates for states in different areas as laid down in Schedule A are inserted here.

DISTRICT	MINIMUM INSIDE SKILLED LABOR		MINIMUM OUTSIDE COMMON LABOR	
	DOLLARS PER DAY	CENTS PER HOUR	DOLLARS PER DAY	CENTS PER HOUR
Pennsylvania	$4.60	57½	$3.60	45
Alabama	3.40	42½	2.40	30
Montana	5.63	70	4.82	60¼

from *The New Deal and Business Recovery*]

Article V—Conditions of Employment

(a) Employees shall have the right to organize and bargain collectively through representatives of their own choosing, and shall be free from the interference, restraint, or coercion of employers of labor, or their agents, in the designation of such representatives or in self-organization or in other concerted activities for the purpose of collective bargaining or other mutual aid or protection; (1) no employee and no one seeking employment shall be required as a condition of employment to join a company union or to refrain from joining, organizing, or assisting a labor organization of his own choosing; and (2) employers shall comply with the maximum hours of labor, minimum rates of pay, and other conditions of employment approved or prescribed by the President. . . .

(f) No person under seventeen (17) years of age shall be employed inside any mine or in hazardous occupations outside any mine, provided, however, that where a state law provides a higher minimum age, the state law shall govern; no person under the age of sixteen (16) shall be employed in or about a mine. . . .

Article VI—Unfair Practices

Section I. The selling of coal under a fair market price (necessary to carry out the purposes of the National Industrial Recovery Act, to pay the minimum rates herein established, and to furnish employment for labor) is hereby declared to be an unfair competitive practice and in violation of this Code. In order to determine the fair market price, agencies shall be established, as hereinafter provided, and sales of coal at any time at price . . . [for] less than a fair market price determined and published, as hereinafter provided, shall create against any person selling at a lower price a prima facie presumption that such a person is engaged in destructive price cutting and unfair competition.

Article VII—Administration

. . . Sec. 4. *Industrial Board.*—There shall be established within ten days after the creation of the Divisional Code Authorities a National Bituminous Coal Industrial Board . . . . This Board shall have the duties and exercise the powers conferred upon it in this Code . . . and to make recommendations to the Divisional Code Authorities and to the President as to any amendments of this Code, or other measures which may stabilize and improve the conditions of the industry and promote the public interest therein.

III

F.D.R. ON INDUSTRIAL HARMONY

On September 30, 1934, President Roosevelt, in one of his many "fireside chats" to the nation over radio, outlined his expectations for improved relations between labor and management. □ From *The Public Papers and Addresses of Franklin D. Roosevelt,* by Franklin D. Roosevelt, Vol. 3, pp. 413–420. Copyright © 1938 by Franklin D. Roosevelt. Reprinted by permission of Random House, Inc.

Recently the most notable public questions that have concerned us all have had to do with industry and labor and with respect to these, certain developments have taken place which I consider of importance. I am happy to report that after years of uncertainty, culminating in the collapse of the spring of 1933, we are bringing order out of the old chaos with a greater certainty of the employment of labor at a reasonable wage and of more business at a fair profit. These governmental and industrial developments hold promise of new achievements for the Nation.

Men may differ as to the particular form of governmental activity with respect to industry and business, but nearly all are agreed that private enterprise in times such as these cannot be left without assistance and without reasonable safeguards lest it destroy not only itself but also our processes of civilization. The underlying necessity for such activity is indeed as strong now as it was years ago when Elihu Root said the following very significant words:

"Instead of the give and take of free individual contract, the tremendous power of organization has combined great aggregations of capital in enormous industrial establishments working through vast agencies of commerce and employing great masses of men in movements of production and transportation and trade, so great in the mass that each individual concerned in them is quite helpless by himself. The relations between the employer and the employed, between the owners of aggregated capital and the units of organized labor, between the small producer, the small trader, the consumer, and the great transporting and manufacturing and distributing agencies, all present new questions for the solution of which the old reliance upon the free action of individual wills appears quite inadequate. And in many directions, the intervention of that organized control which we call government seems necessary to produce the same result of justice and right conduct which obtained through the attrition of individuals before the new conditions arose. . . ."

In meeting the problems of industrial recovery the chief agency of the Government has been the National Recovery Administration. Under its guidance, trades and industries covering over 90 percent of all industrial employees have adopted codes of fair competition, which have been approved by the President. Under these codes, in the industries covered, child labor has been eliminated. The work day and the work week have been shortened. Minimum wages have been established and other wages adjusted toward a rising standard of living. The emergency purpose of the N.R.A. was to put men to work and since its creation more than four million persons have been reemployed, in great part through the cooperation of American business brought about under the codes.

Benefits of the Industrial Recovery Program have come, not only to labor in the form of new jobs, in relief from overwork and in relief from underpay, but also to the owners and managers of industry because, together with a great increase in the payrolls, there has come a substantial rise in the total of industrial profits—a rise from a deficit figure in the first quarter of 1933 to a level of sustained profits within one year from the inauguration of N.R.A.

Now it should not be expected that even employed labor and capital would be completely satisfied with present conditions. Employed workers have not by any means all enjoyed a return to the earnings of prosperous times, although millions of hitherto underprivileged workers are today far better paid than ever before. Also, billions of dollars of invested capital have today a greater security of present and future earning power than before. This is because of the establishment of fair, competitive standards and because of relief from unfair competition in wage cutting which depresses markets and destroys purchasing power. But it is an undeniable fact that the restoration of other billions of sound investments to a reasonable earning power could not be brought about in one year. There is no magic formula, no economic panacea, which would simply revive overnight the heavy industries and the trades dependent upon them. . . .

During the last twelve months our industrial recovery has been to some extent retarded by strikes, including a few of major importance. I would not minimize the inevitable losses to employers and employees and to the general public through such conflicts. But I would point out that the extent and severity of labor disputes during this period have been far less than in any previous comparable period.

When the business men of the country were demanding the right to organize themselves adequately to promote their legitimate interest; when the farmers were demanding legislation which would give them opportunities and incentives to organize themselves for a common advance, it was natural that the workers should seek and obtain a statutory declaration of their constitutional right to organize themselves for collective bargaining as embodied in Section 7-A of the National Industrial Recovery Act.

Machinery set up by the Federal Government has provided some new methods of adjustment. Both employers and employees must share the blame of not using them as fully as they should. The employer who turns away from impartial agencies of peace, who denies freedom of organization to his employees, or fails to make every reasonable effort at a peaceful solution of their differences, is not fully supporting the recovery effort of his Government. The workers who turn away from these same impartial agencies and decline to use their good offices to gain their ends are likewise not fully cooperating with their Government.

It is time that we made a clean-cut effort to bring about that united action of management and labor, which is one of the high purposes of the Recovery Act. We have passed through more than a year of education. Step by step we have created all the Government agencies necessary to insure, as a general rule, industrial peace, with justice for all those willing to use these agencies whenever their voluntary bargaining fails to produce a necessary agreement.

There should be at least a full and fair trial given to these means of ending industrial warfare; and in such an effort we should be able to secure for employers and employees and consumers the benefits that all derive from the continuous, peaceful operation of our essential enterprises.

IV

THE NATIONAL LABOR RELATIONS ACT

After the N.I.R.A. was declared unconstitutional, Congress enacted the National Labor Relations Act, commonly known as the Wagner Act. It incorporated many of the provisions of the N.I.R.A. affecting labor. This reading raises some questions about the validity of the basic assumptions underlying the Wagner Act. □ Reprinted from *The National Labor Relations Act,* by William H. Spencer, pp. 1–3. By permission of The University of Chicago Press. Copyright © 1935 by the University of Chicago.

The Seventy-fourth Congress enacted and the President of the United States on July 5, 1935, approved the National Labor Relations Act. While it was under consideration in Congress, organized labor stood solidly for the law; employers stood stolidly against it.

This legislation was enacted to carry out the vaguely stated policy of Section I of the Norris-LaGuardia Anti-injunction Act of 1932, and the policy of the preamble and Section 7 (a) of the National Industrial Recovery Act of 1933. The provisions of this legislation, however, go beyond those of Section 7 (a) of the Recovery Act, even as interpreted by the old National Labor Relations Board. The Act restates the rights of workers with respect to self-organization and collective bargaining. For the protection of these rights it defines certain unfair labor practices with sharpness and precision. It creates—or continues—the National Labor Relations Board. It empowers the Labor Board to assist employees in the selection and designation of representatives for purposes of collective bargaining, and gives it quasi-judicial powers in the field of unfair labor practices comparable to those exercised by the Federal Trade Commision in the field of unfair market practices. . . .

Employers, whether or not they like the law—and they most assuredly do not like it—must make their adjustments to it. Employees, although for the time being pleased with the law, also face serious problems of adjustment. It may safely be predicted that for a year—perhaps for a longer period —the nation will witness much maneuvering, scheming, and industrial strife as employers and employees, under the supervision of the Labor Board, make their adjustments under this most recent endeavor of the government "to promote equality of bargaining between employers and employees." . . .

In the first place, the legislation proceeds on the assumption that employers enjoy a substantial advantage over individual employees in the negotiations of terms of employment, and that this advantage "arises out of the organization of employers in corporate forms of ownership and out of numerous other modern industrial conditions."

It is assumed, in the second place, that "the inequality of bargaining power between employees who do not possess full freedom of association or actual liberty of contract, and employers who are organized in the corporate or other forms of ownership association substantially burdens and affects the flow of commerce, and tends to aggravate recurrent business depressions by depressing wage rates and the purchasing power of wage earners in industry and by preventing the stabilization of competitive wage rates and working conditions within and between industries."

In the third place, the legislation is based on the assumption that "the denial by employers of the right of employees to organize and the refusal by employers to accept the procedure of collective bargaining lead to strikes and other forms of industrial strife or unrest, which have the intent or the necessary effect of burdening or obstructing commerce" in various ways.

In the fourth place, the legislation assumes that equality of bargaining power between employers and employees as to wages, hours, and basic working conditions will (1) tend to increase the purchasing power of employees by making it possible for them to exact higher wages from employers, thus lessening the impact of business depressions; (2) tend to foster, protect, and promote commerce among the several states; and (3) tend to lessen industrial strife.

Finally, the legislation proceeds on the assumption—not explicit, of course, but certainly implicit—that we are in a collectivist era; that, since capital is typically highly organized, labor must be encouraged to organize; and that the possibility of returning to a régime of competition is remote, if not entirely out of the question.

PROBLEM 12

Rise of the C.I.O.

Although labor enjoyed a friendly governmental atmosphere and favorable legislation during the early 1930's, industrial strife by no means disappeared during the decade. In 1934, a record year for strikes, workingmen turned to unions in unprecedented numbers. A small and militant group of labor leaders helped to attract a growing membership but, at the same time, were instrumental in creating a major rift in the ranks of union organizations.

Just as the principles of organization underlying the Knights of Labor had been challenged by the emerging American Federation of Labor in the nineteenth century, so in turn were basic premises of the A.F. of L. questioned and then abandoned by this new leadership. The Knights had fostered one large union of diverse membership while the creators of the A.F. of L. favored closely knit organization along strictly craft lines. In the twentieth century the question debated concerned the need to organize workers in industry-wide unions, regardless of their special crafts.

The main targets of this new union effort were the mass production industries involving steel, automobiles, rubber products, and electrical appliances. At first, the A.F. of L. undertook to organize workers temporarily in these fields into unaffiliated "federal unions" with the intention of eventually reassigning them to specific craft unions, already in existence, which claimed jurisdiction. Resistance to this program developed within the A.F. of L., and John L. Lewis, leader of the United Mine Workers, emerged as the spokesman of the opposition group. Lewis and his supporters contended that it was futile to seek to organize a basic industry along craft lines. They favored "industrial unionism" in which the union structure would correspond to the structure of the industry with which the workers were dealing.

At the 1934 national convention of the A.F. of L. a group of craft-union presidents attempted to obtain approval for a plan to organize workers in certain mass production industries into industrial unions. They were defeated, but far from discouraged. Led by John L. Lewis, this faction made another attempt at Atlantic City in 1935. In a vote of historic consequence the convention delegates again resisted the attempt to establish industrial unionism.

Undaunted, Lewis and seven other union leaders established a Committee for Industrial Organization to work within the A.F. of L. and to organize the basic industries. At this point the A.F. of L. asked the Committee to disband. Lewis and his group refused to obey, and the unions affiliated with the Committee were suspended from the A.F. of L.

In November 1935 Lewis and the suspended unions opened offices in Washington and announced their intention to launch a massive drive to organize the unorganized. Successful sit-down strikes in several industries and a peacefully negotiated contract with the United States Steel Corporation in 1937 gave the new group added prestige and power. The next year it held a constitutional convention and emerged as the Congress of Industrial Organizations (C.I.O.). At the end of 1938 its membership exceeded that of the A.F. of L.

The readings which follow are designed to show the nature and purposes of the C.I.O., its techniques of organization, and the spirit of the time in which it emerged. As you read, think of these questions:

1 "The tactics used by the C.I.O. indicate that its leaders profited from the mistakes made by organized labor during the unsuccessful steel strike of 1919." What evidence is there to support this statement?

2 On what ground does John L. Lewis base his charge that the A.F. of L. failed to meet the needs of American workers?

3 Why did the sit-down strikes succeed? What was the role of the government? of public opinion? of the New Deal legislation?

4 What accounted for the success of the S.W.O.C.? What part did government play in this success?

I

JOHN L. LEWIS ON INDUSTRIAL UNIONISM

In a convention speech highly critical of the organizing policies of the American Federation of Labor, John L. Lewis attempted to show assembled delegates the need for industrial unions. The following excerpts are from the report of proceedings of the 1935 national meeting of the A. F. of L. at Atlantic City, New Jersey. ☐ *Report of Proceedings, American Federation of Labor*, Vol. 55, pp. 534, 535–536, 539, 540–541, 542. Copyright © 1935.

I have had perhaps as much experience in organizing workers in the various industries as any member of the Executive Council of the American Federation of Labor or any officer thereof. I served an apprenticeship of five and one-half years as a general organizer for the American Federation of Labor before I became an officer of the United Mine Workers of America. During that period of time I worked in the steel industry, the rubber industry, the glass industry, the lumber industry, the copper industry, and other industries in most of the states of this Union.

Then, as now, the American Federation of Labor offered to the workers in these industries a plan of organization into Federal labor unions or local trade unions with the understanding that when organized they would be segregated into the various organizations of their respective crafts. . . .

What is the record? Delegate Howard expressed it when he said that we laid claim to a membership of approximately three and a half million, out of an organizable number of approximately thirty-nine million. There is the answer. If we know nothing else on the question we can at least read the results, and in reading the results we surely understand that our influence is less great . . . than it would be if we had those twenty-five million workers that President Green [of the A.F. of L.], in his public address in 1934, talked of organizing. Where are they? Where are those twenty-five million that in a moment of exuberance we were going to organize? Perhaps President Green's arithmetic was wrong and he meant twenty-five thousand, because the total results are nearer the twenty-five thousand than the twenty-five million. . . .

I submit it to be a reasonable statement that it will be a long time before the American Federation of Labor organizes those 25,000,000 workers that we are all so anxious to organize. There are others among us who believe that the record indicates a need for a change in policy. This convention floor is teeming with delegates from those industries where those local unions have been established and where they are now dying like the grass withering before the Autumn sun, who are ready to tell this convention of the need for that change in policy.

Those of us who have had experience in these mass production industries are ready to state our professional judgment for what it may be worth and say that it is an absolute fact that America's great modern industries cannot be successfully organized and those organizations maintained against the power of the adversaries of labor in this country under the policy which has been followed for the last quarter of a century in dealing with that subject.

There has been a change in industry, a constant daily change in its processes, a constant change in its employment conditions, a great concentration of opposition to the extension and the logical expansion of the trade union movement. Great combinations of capital have assembled great industrial plants, and they are strung across the borders of our several states from the north to the south and from the east to the west in such a manner that they have assembled to themselves tremendous power and influence, and they are almost 100 per cent effective in opposing organization of the workers under the policies of the American Federation of Labor.

What are we going to do about it? . . .

We hesitate, perhaps, because there are men here representing great organizations that have rendered a splendid service to their membership formed, on craft lines, who fear that such a policy would jeopardize the interests of their members and jeopardize the interests of their own positions. Their unions are already jeopardized and their membership is already jeopardized because unless the American Federation of Labor may be successful in organizing these unorganized workers, it is extremely doubtful whether many of these organizations now so perfect, now so efficient, will long be permitted to endure and to function in a manner that is conducive to the well-being of their membership. . . .

The average worker . . . does not need to be told that a trade union or labor organization is of advantage to him if he is given the privilege of being a member of it under circumstances that he can accept. . . .

I am telling you facts and I am telling you what is in the hearts of my people, and my people down in Alabama tonight are hungry as I stand talking here, because the Tennessee Coal & Iron Co. is daring enough and bold enough to close their mines to them. And I might say to you that because of circumstances in Alabama prevailing in several counties there is no adequate system of public relief there or Government relief, and our people are suffering, and they are suffering, in its final essence, by the fact that the American Federation of Labor, for some reason or other, has failed after all these years of experimentation to organize the iron and steel workers and establish collective bargaining in that industry.

How long does any one think the United Mine Workers of America will be satisfied with that policy? . . .

What of the future of our country? Who among us that does not know the hazards of the present moment? The teachings of false prophets falling upon the ears of a population that is frightened and disturbed and depressed and discouraged, the nocturnal and surreptitious attempts of interests to form a philosophy, the philosophy of the Communists on the one hand and the philosophy of the Nazis on the other hand, equally repugnant and distasteful to the men of labor. And yet it is constituting a serious, deadly menace for the future.

Not one man here but knows that American labor in its declared policies stands for a course that provides for the acceptance of neither the one philosophy nor the other, but a course that will protect our form of government and our established institutions, and a form of government that will take into consideration the needs and requirements of every-day Americans, the common people, if you please, and the common people of this country are the people who work for a living. The American Federation of Labor stands for that. How much more security would we have in this country for the future for our form of government if we had a virile labor movement that represented, not merely a cross-section of skilled workers, but that represented the men who work with their hands in our great industries, regardless of their trade and calling. . . .

Is it right, after all, that because some of us are capable of forging great and powerful organizations of skilled craftsmen in this country that we should lock ourselves up in our own domain and say, "I am merely working for those who pay me"? Isn't it right that we should contribute something of our own strength, our own virtues, our own knowledge, our own influence toward those less fortunately situated, in the knowledge that if we help them and they grow strong, in turn that we will be the beneficiary of their changed status and their strength? The strength of a strong man is a prideful thing, but the unfortunate thing in life is that strong men do not remain strong. And that is just as true of unions and labor organizations as it is true of men and individuals. . . .

. . . The enemies of labor in this country will be encouraged and high wassail will prevail at the banquet tables of the mighty throughout the country if the American Federation of Labor refuses to grant the petition of these industries that are fighting for the objectives of labor and to defend the rights of mankind.

II

GENERAL MOTORS WORKERS SIT DOWN

Although it did not survive as a weapon of organized labor, the sit-down strikes of the 1930's gave the C.I.O. a new technique in its struggle against management. Following is an account of the strike at the Flint, Michigan, plant of General Motors in January 1937. □ *Labor in America,* by Foster Rhea Dulles, pp. 303–306. Copyright 1949, 1955 © 1960 by Foster Rhea Dulles. Thomas Y. Crowell Company, New York, publishers.

This strike was something new under the sun. It took the form in Flint of a sit-down. There had been some earlier use of this radical technique, notably among the rubber workers at Akron, but the General Motors strike marked its first use on a really wide scale. The automobile workers refused to leave the plant; they just sat at their work benches. It was not an act of violence but one of passive resistance, doubly effective in that such a strike could be broken only by the forcible removal of the workers from company premises. . . .

The C.I.O. at first looked upon the strike with misgivings and was anything but enthusiastic over the sit-down. Deeply involved in the organizing drive in steel, whose success was considered basic to the whole program of industrial unionism, the outbreak in automobiles was highly embarrassing. But support could not be withheld and the C.I.O. undertook to do everything it could to aid the General Motors employes. "You men are undoubtedly carrying on through one of the most heroic battles that has ever been undertaken by strikers in an industrial dispute," Lewis declared. "The attention of the entire American public is focussed upon you. . . ."

The latter part of his statement was unquestionably true, and became even more so as violence broke out in Flint and the strikers showed their stubborn determination not be be dislodged from the occupied plants. The cutting off of all heat—even though it was the dead of winter—made no difference. When the police tried to rush Fisher Body Plant No. 2, they were met by a hail of missiles—coffee mugs, pop bottles, iron bolts and heavy automobile door hinges. When they then returned to the attack with tear-gas bombs, the strikers retaliated by turning streams of water on them from the plant fire hoses. The forces of law and order were finally compelled to make a hasty retreat in what the exultant workers promptly termed the "Battle of the Running Bulls."

The strike dragged on from week to week as the General Motors employes continued to sit it out with food and other supplies brought in to them through the picket lines. Discipline was rigid. "Brilliantly lighted," reads a contemporary description by a union organizer, "this vast plant was heavily guarded inside and outside—to keep strikebreakers and other interlopers from entering and to protect the building and its contents. Especially did these strikers guard the company's dies. . . . Forty-five men were assigned to police patrol duty inside. . . ."

Both the company and the Flint Alliance [a company-sponsored association] now demanded that the state militia be mobilized to clear the plants since the police had failed to do so. But Governor Murphy of Michigan, sympathetic with the automobile workers and fearful of the bloodshed that would certainly result, refused to take this step. Finally, however, General Motors obtained a court order setting 3:00 P.M. on February 3 as the deadline for evacuation of the plants under penalty of imprisonment and fines. The strikers were undismayed. "We the workers," they wired the governor, ". . . have carried on a stay-in strike over a month to make General Motors Corporation obey the law and engage in collective bargaining. . . . Unarmed as we are, the introduction of the militia, sheriffs or police with murderous weapons will mean a blood-bath of unarmed workers. . . . We have decided to stay in the plant."

Realizing that the strikers meant what they said, Murphy frantically summoned a peace conference. John L. Lewis rushed to Detroit . . . .

The zero hour approached—and passed. Governor Murphy refused to order the national guardsmen to enforce the court order. In spite of mounting popular pressure, he remained unwilling to make a move that would have precipitated violence on an unpredictable scale.

The next day President Roosevelt added his request for a continuation of negotiations to that of Governor Murphy, and the Lewis-Knudsen talks (with other representatives of both General Motors and the strikers present) were resumed. For a full week, while the sit-downers grimly held the fort, the conference proceeded until at long last, the weary, haggard governor was able to announce that agreement had been reached. General Motors undertook to recognize the United Automobile Workers as the bargaining agent for its members, to drop injunction proceedings against the strikers, not to discriminate in any way against union members, and to take up such grievances as the speed-up and other matters.

. . . Organized labor had taken the first step toward what was to become the complete unionization of the entire automobile industry. Whatever might be said of the legality or ethics of a sit-down strike, the results spoke for its effectiveness.

III

ORGANIZING INDUSTRIAL WORKERS

An important reason for the success of the C.I.O. was its aggressive methods of organizing workers. The next selection describes techniques used by the Steel Workers' Organizing Committee (S.W.O.C.) under its chairman, Philip Murray, who was also vice-president of the United Mine Workers. ☐ Herbert Harris, "How the C.I.O. Works," *Current History,* May 1937, pp. 61, 62–66.

The night shift comes out of the mill into the yard, into the dripping grayness of an early morning in Pittsburgh. . . .

Smiting their ears, the metallic lungs of a sound truck (rolling into action some 20 feet in front of them) send a slogan "Be Wise. Organize" into a pea-soup sky, piercing it with rhythmic rising insistence. . . .

At the gates, with black slickers glinting in the drear uncertain light, stand two men who hand out leaflets as the steel workers emerge, and who urge in stage-whisper tones: "You ought to join up, buddy"—"Read this and use your head"—"You ought to be with us for your own good"—"We're going to win this time"—"You can trust the C.I.O. . . ."

But before any such out-in-the-open onslaught could begin, the S.W.O.C. miners and sappers had first to weaken the walls. And they, like the rest, were guided by the canny Philip Murray, vice president of the United Mine Workers and chairman of the S.W.O.C. . . .

It must be remembered that the C.I.O. High Command, from the very first, proceeded on the theory that if steel could be forced to yield to collective bargaining the whole industrial front could be more readily captured. . . . [The] C.I.O. gambled all of its might in money and men, in political pressures and persuasions, upon the success or failure of the S.W.O.C. drive. To Mr. Lewis it was to be Austerlitz or Waterloo. . . .

Murray was equipped for his job. Due largely to his own organizing talents, exercised over a period of 29 years, the United Mine Workers with its membership of 540,000 has grown into the strongest union in North America. He grew up among men who must earn their bread in the callouses of their hands, in the sweat of their collective brow. . . . He joined the Madison local of the U.M.W., devoting himself to its expansion. Gregarious by nature, liking to talk with people, to draw them out, he proved an excellent missionary for the union faith. At 18 he was elected president of his own local of 750 men. . . .

At 50 Murray radiates a quiet vitality. . . . He speaks slowly, thoughtfully, with a Scotch burr. . . . He dresses like a small-town banker—blue suit, blue tie, black shoes, gray overcoat and hat to match.

The need for complete unity in purpose, in program, in personnel was among his chief concerns when on July 1, 1936, the first $500,000 for the S.W.O.C. offensive had been raised by the U.M.W. . . . Encouraged by the amount of his ammunition and, like all Scotsmen, determined to make every penny count, Murray set up headquarters in the very heart of steel, in Pittsburgh. He rented a suite of offices on the 36th floor of the Grant Building, which houses more of steel's officialdom than any other building in the country. . . .

Like a good general he surrounded himself with an able, resourceful staff. As Regional Director for the Pittsburgh area, he selected lanky, gray-haired Clinton S. Golden, former locomotive engineer, chicken-farmer, and one-time New Deal representative for the N.L.R.B. For Golden's right and left bowers, Mr. Murray installed smart, scrappy Lee Pressman, quondam attorney for Mr. Hopkins' W.P.A., and the knowing, quick-witted Vincent Sweeney, quondam star reporter for the Pittsburgh *Press*.

Among Mr. Golden's first functions was to persuade Michael Francis Tighe, oak-hearted pilot of the ill-fated Amalgamated Union of Iron, Steel, and Tin Workers to relinquish the steering-wheel to the S.W.O.C. crew. And on September 3, 1936, Mr. Tighe—symbol of an old passing order in labor things—resigned his post, taking with him many ghosts of those "jurisdictional disputes" which had haunted and hindered unionism in steel for a generation. While this obstacle to closer harmony was being removed, Mr. Pressman concentrated on ways and means of cracking wide open various city ordinances in company towns which sought to prohibit such "union activities" as the exercise of free speech and freedom of assembly. Mr. Sweeney started to establish friendly relations with editors, correspondents for news services, radio commentators, ministers, educators, politicians and many other people who, in one way or another, could influence public opinion and help to whip up sympathy for the S.W.O.C. and its aims. He also dug diligently into files of complaints from steel workers, complaints ranging from overlong hours to defective smoke glasses, and boots and gloves which, supplied by the company, weren't properly treated with chemicals to withstand heat and prevent discomfort and burns. Grievances which might strike a recognition spark of "why, that's my trouble, too" were boiled down into pamphlets of simple prose.

"The most difficult thing, we were up against," said Mr. Murray recently in an exclusive *Current History* interview, "was an intangible. It was fear—fear of fellow-workers, of foremen, of superintendents, of neighbors—for in

most steel plants even a kind word about a union meant loss of your job—
and a probable black-listing, besides. . . ."

The 150 organizers dispatched to steel's four corners by Mr. Murray
. . . told puddlers, rollers, and the rest that "times" were different, that
their hour had come. During the first stages of the S.W.O.C. drive, in furtive
gatherings in dingy halls, a speaker would end his exhortation with a punch-
line gesture sure to bring down the house. He would cross his middle and
index finger, lean confidentially towards his audience and say: "And I tell
you, boys, John L. Lewis and President Roosevelt, why, they're just like
that," and he would hold his entwined fingers high in the air until the full
import of his remark sank in. . . .

In Pennsylvania, S.W.O.C. organizers proved their contention that times
had changed in dramatic fashion. Lieutenant Governor of the Quaker State
was, and is, Thomas Kennedy, a U.M.W. member and an ardent unionist.
Often S.W.O.C. emissaries called on him to supply State troopers to protect
their squadrons from unduly hostile local authorities. It was a common sight
in Pennsylvania, especially during the fall and winter of 1936-37, to see State
troopers, armed to the teeth, preserving law and order in steel towns while
S.W.O.C. orators proclaimed the new day from street corners or sound-
trucks. . . .

. . . At the outset, Mr. Murray and his aides sought mainly to interest
former members of the Amalgamated Union, or others with union background such as mine-workers who had left the pit for puddling. And to ward
off suspicion of group gatherings a S.W.O.C. organizer would ask a new con-
vert to hold a raffle at his home. While the lucky numbers were drawn and
the women gossiped, a man here, another there, was taken in a corner and
sold the S.W.O.C. program. He was then asked to suggest the names of
other prospects. By this means an "active list" was quickly built up. Sometimes, of course, a poker party or a horseshoes tournament in a backyard
served as rallying point for potential S.W.O.C. adherents. Dues were one
dollar a month for the employed. The jobless were admitted without charge.
All income from dues was ploughed back into the locality whence it came and
used for hiring a hall, for printing handbills, and the like. As soon as a new
member signed his card, it was mailed hastily to headquarters in Pittsburgh
to guard against a "raid" of an organizer's hotel-room upon some trumped-
up charge.

The S.W.O.C. field men next turned to fostering alliances between the
many fraternal societies, the "Lithuanian Lodges," the "Polish Mutual Benefits," and "Czechoslovakian Sokols," along with church groups and card
clubs and even Legion Posts. At the outset a series of conventions was held

in every community. Every segment of steel's working populace, racial and religious, was represented by its own delegates. . . .

Last but not least on the S.W.O.C. schedule was the maneuver to win over and absorb the company unions. When section 7a of the N.I.R.A. promised a new era in collective bargaining, steel was among the first industries to set up such employee representation groups to evade any independent unionism. From the employers' standpoint, it was a mistake. The company union, despite all its restrictions of management control, taught the men to act in concert. It taught them to formulate demands. It taught them parliamentary procedure. It "gave them ideas. . . ."

To crystallize this atmosphere of discontent Mr. Murray sent out word that the S.W.O.C. would be glad to help company union chieftains in gaining their goals. The S.W.O.C. legal division would be delighted to supply pointers in questions of law. The research department would be equally pleased to furnish facts and figures on how much a particular steel corporation paid in dividends last year, the size of official salaries and bonuses, and the amount of its capital reserves. At the same time, leaders of company unions were buttonholed, beered-with, brought into the S.W.O.C. line of thinking. A number of them came over bag and baggage to the S.W.O.C. by the end of summer, 1936. Then at a conference of company union groups on September 16, 1936, it was voted to help the S.W.O.C. gain control of the two most powerful employee representation units: the Calumet Central Committee (Chicago) and the Pittsburgh Central Committee. When this result was achieved by special elections, lobbyings, and borings from within, a joint board representing both Calumet and Pittsburgh bodies, and studded with S.W.O.C. advisers, was ready for business. It promptly adopted a new wage program asking a five dollar per day minimum for common labor as against the four dollar per day that had just been established by steel corporations to "ward off the menace of the C.I.O., and the communism of John L. Lewis."

This basic demand was followed up by others asking strict enforcement of seniority rights, vacations with pay, protective provisions such as better ventilation, and recognition of this S.W.O.C.-controlled joint board as the collective bargaining agency.

"We kept them constantly biting at the heels of management," says Mr. Murray, "for these concessions. We made certain of one thing—facts. We triple-checked our facts on company earnings, and ability to pay higher wages."

At about this point, coinciding with Roosevelt's re-election, Mr. Murray decided that the days of quietness were over, and that the day of skirling bagpipes had arrived. . . .

From the late fall of 1936 through the turn of the year, the S.W.O.C. let go with everything it had: rallies, speakers, leaflets, pamphlets, posters, radio broadcasts, meetings in the street, at home, in a bar, conferences and parades to celebrate again the victories of various "labor candidates" at the polls. The response was overwhelming. Nearly 2,000 new members a day began swamping the facilities of S.W.O.C. regional offices.

Speeding into steel towns where to mention union was a heresy went cars carrying S.W.O.C. flying squadrons. On many occasions they were accompanied by special investigators from Washington, D.C. with banners draped over the hood of their automobiles and carrying the legend:

"CAR OF THE UNITED STATES SENATE"
LA FOLLETTE CIVIL LIBERTIES COMMITTEE
Investigators

Local authorities—policemen, sheriffs, company guards—took a long hard look at this cavalcade and sighed. It was impossible to shoot, club, or tear-gas this aggregation. For all they knew they might hurt a Senator . . . .

On March 2, 1937, Carnegie-Illinois signed its famous agreement with the S.W.O.C., ending an era.

Today Mr. Murray's organization numbers 275,000 out of the 450,000 workers in steel. And it was the S.W.O.C. "acid-tested" tactics that are now the model and maxim for C.I.O.'s organizing drives in textiles, in oil, in aluminum, and in other mass production spheres.

Back of Mr. Murray and the S.W.O.C., of course, were John L. Lewis and the 15 unions of the C.I.O. with all its far-reaching power and prestige. Both that power and prestige derive from a new labor philosophy, the "industrial idea," the essence of which is that the vertical, centralized holding-company control over industry must be met by the same kind of control over labor. A first premise of this outlook is that the monopolies of the "Big Money" must be matched in economic and political strength by mobilizing masses of men. It is an outlook which, as embodied in the C.I.O., spurns the derby-wearing, cigar-chewing, "I'm tough, see," walking delegate of a bygone day and all that he symbolized. It insists on brimming coffers. It hires first-rate brains. It stream-lines its strategy. It makes a fetish of efficiency. In every respect, it emulates the structure of Big Business, fighting it with its own weapons, and propelled by a kind of crusading zeal that portends profound changes in the relationship between capital and labor in the United States.

PROBLEM 13

Abuses of Economic Power

The means employed by the contending groups to promote their causes is one of the most interesting aspects of the struggle between labor and management in the United States. These methods have changed over the years according to stages of economic development, shifting power relationships of labor and management, and prevailing attitudes of the government. In the interaction of government, labor, and management the use of violence and other unusual means of achieving important aims has been a recurring problem.

The readings included in Problem 13 illuminate incidents and policies in which both labor and management have been involved in controversial practices.

In both the Haymarket affair and the Great Steel Strike of 1919, government itself was open to criticism because of the tactics it used in labor disputes.

During the nineteenth and early twentieth centuries, the greater portion of violence in labor affairs seems to have originated with management. In recent years publicity has been concentrated on the illegal practices of labor unions.

Very often the emotionally charged atmosphere of a labor controversy has resulted in an exchange of recriminations by union leaders and employers who have accused each other of startling and even brutal crimes. In some cases these charges have proved to be false; often they have been all too true. The activities of the racketeer who uses labor disputes and organizations for personal gain have been especially disturbing. In the early history of the labor movement, the private detective agency drew lucrative commissions by providing strikebreakers, spies, and strong-arm hoodlums to management. On the other side, the corrupt union business agent attempted to feather his own nest by extorting payments from employers who wished to avoid trouble.

The growth of the labor movement since the 1930's has created a prominent national issue of corruption and racketeering in the labor-management field.

The La Follette Civil Liberties Committee, a Congressional investigating body, shocked the nation in the late 1930's with its revelations of violent methods used against unions by some employers. Senator John L. McClellan, in another exposé, during the 1950's, made equally sensational headlines by proving that organized crime had infiltrated and even taken over a number of labor organizations.

The readings which follow are designed to present a picture of the problem of corruption and crime in labor history. As you read, consider the following questions:

1   In your opinion, why did some of the large corporations engage private agencies to intervene in labor quarrels? Do you think that the presence in some labor unions of radicals and agitators justified management's recourse to such organizations as the "Bergoff Army" and the Pinkerton Agency? Explain.

2   What does the author of Reading II mean when he says that "labor racketeering is but a symptom of a far larger problem"? Do you agree? Why, or why not?

3   How do you account for the strong support which some unions have given to men such as Dave Beck and James Hoffa? Do you believe that corruption is an inevitable outgrowth of big labor? On what do you base your opinion?

4   Compare the tone of the selections by George Meany and James Carey. Do you think that these two men are saying essentially the same thing?

5   How would Meany and Carey probably respond to the recommendations of Senator Kennedy in the final reading?

I

AN ARMY OF STRIKEBREAKERS

One of the most elaborate organizations furnishing employers with personnel trained to forcibly intervene in strikes was the "Bergoff Army." This agency sent potential clients a detailed prospectus describing its various "services." In the following selection, the writer tears down the façade of words in the prospectus and attempts to describe the true nature of the Bergoff organization. ☐ Edward Levinson, *I Break Strikes!* pp. 52–54, 55–57. New York: Robert M. McBride and Co., copyright © 1935.

By 1909 the Bergoff army had become a fairly regularized host. . . . They were not, of course, a standing army. Rather were they mustered anew as each strike was called. . . .

Bergoff has divided his warriors into several classifications, indicating the variety of services he is prepared to offer, and the specialists who are available for their execution. With little variation during the last twenty-eight years, he has enumerated these specialists in a prospectus designed for the eyes of business executives. The current edition of this document describes five categories of experts:

STRIKE PREVENTION DEPARTMENT

This department is composed of men possessing natural leadership qualifications. Men of intelligence, courage, and great persuasive powers to counteract the evil influence of strike agitators and the radical element.

UNDERCOVER DEPARTMENT

Our undercover department is composed of carefully selected male and female mechanics and workpeople. They furnish accurate information of the movements and contemplated actions of their fellow employees —"Forewarned is forearmed."

OPENSHOP LABOR DEPARTMENT

This department is composed of an organization equipped to supply all classes of competent mechanics and workpeople to keep the wheels of industry moving during a strike.

PROTECTION DEPARTMENT

This department is composed of big, disciplined men with military or police experience, for the protection of life and property.

INVESTIGATION DEPARTMENT

Our investigation department is international in scope and embraces all branches. The personnel is composed of male and female operatives of the highest calibre.

Within the profession less formal descriptions are used. The Openshop Department deals in finks, the bottom of the scale in strikebreaking. Above them are the guards, armed and unarmed, who make up the Protection Department. In keeping with their elevated positions, they are known as "nobles." Between the finks and the nobles are the "boots" who constitute the personnel of the Strike Prevention and Undercover departments. . . .

Casting about for a word to express adequately their loathing of the professional strikebreakers, the Industrial Workers of the World and, soon after, other trade unionists, selected "fink" as the proper description. The term was borrowed from the criminal world where fink, as a verb, means to turn informer, to betray, to squeal. A second interpretation defines a fink as "a criminal who is dissatisfied with his loot." The inspiration of the I.W.W. came from the verb, and gave to it a new meaning—one who betrays his fellow workers by scabbing for money. . . .

The nobles act as overseers as well as guards. Finks are frequently unreliable. Some will enlist as strikebreakers for the sake of free transportation and then try to desert. Others will flee at the first sign of violence, while still others will discover, belatedly, that the jobs for which they signed up are strikebreaking affairs. In these cases, the nobles have the additional duty of keeping the finks in line. During the 1912 strike of New York's hotel waiters and cooks, Bergoff signed a contract with the Holland House which illustrates this function. "We also agree," read the pact, "to furnish guards, these men to be thoroughly experienced with strike work and *to do all in their power to prevent all help from deserting their posts* and to conduct this strike on a businesslike basis. . . .

. . . The finks are divided into two large classes. About fifty per cent of them are the "hunger scabs," men who take the work in desperation. To the profession they are the "one-time finks" who sign up for one strike and, for one reason or another, are never seen again. Most of them come from the ranks of the unemployed. Others are too incompetent or too old to hold on to regular jobs. Some are barred from unions because of high dues, or the closing of unions to newcomers. The other half of the finks are shiftless men who do not care to work longer than a week or two at a stretch; adventurers eager for the freebooting of the strikebreaker armies, or criminal types—from petty thieves to murderers—to whom the confusion of a strike offers easy opportunities for looting.

Another prominent private detective agency connected with antiunion activity was the Pinkerton organization. Senator Robert M. La Follette, who investigated violations of civil liberties in industrial relations, offered the following testimony when he appeared before a Senate committee in 1939. □ United States Congress, Senate, Committee on Education and Labor, Hearings, *Oppressive Labor Practices Act,* 76th Congress, 1st Session, pp. 14–15.

The committee first turned its attention to the dirty business of labor spying, which is described in its report on Industrial Espionage. This practice, which is so abhorrent to the American concept of a free society, was found to be flourishing in every quarter. . . .

The leaders in the detective-agency field were summoned to testify. Pinkerton's National Detective Agency, Inc., with offices in 27 cities, was the most powerful dealer in the labor-spy traffic. . . . The clients of Pinkerton's figured among the most powerful corporations in the country. Between 1933 and 1936 Pinkerton had 309 industrial clients, many of them giants in their respective fields of industry, such as the General Motors Corporation, Bethlehem Steel Corporation, Pennsylvania Railroad Co., and Baldwin Locomotive Works.

This blue-ribbon agency employed no less than 1,228 industrial spies between January 1, 1933, and April 1937. More significant, however, than the number of spies at work, the huge sums of money spent for their services, and the list of agency clients, were the facts developed concerning the union affiliations and the position of the spies themselves. This information provided a true index of the extent of the power which professional labor spies wield over the American worker. The facts were truly astounding. Pinkerton operates in practically every union in the country, from the Amalgamated Association of Meat Cutters and Butchers of America to the United Mine Workers of America. Every important international union, many smaller and local unions, even company unions—whether affiliated with the American Federation of Labor, the Congress of Industrial Organizations, or independent, whether craft or industrial—have their quota of Pinkerton spies. Sixty-four Pinkerton operatives have worked within the railroad unions; 17 have held membership in the United Textile Workers of America; 16 have been members of the International Brotherhood of Electrical Workers; 20 have been members of the International Association of Machinists; 52 have held membership in the United Automobile Workers' Union of America; and so the list goes for 93 separate unions. At least 331 of the operatives of the Pinkerton

Detective Agency, according to its own records, have been active union members. Of these at least 100 have held elective offices in unions, one even attaining the position of national vice president of his union. Others serve as presidents of their locals, treasurers, or secretaries, with ready access to the names of the members and to the financial status of the union. Some Pinkerton spies even act as business agents or as organizers of unions.

II

HOW THE LABOR RACKETEER OPERATES

An analysis of the nature of labor racketeering appeared in a report of investigations made by a committee of businessmen of the City Club of New York in 1937. □ Subcommittee on Labor Unions of the Committee on Legislation, *Report on Certain Aspects of Labor Union Responsibility and Control,* pp. 7–8. New York: City Club of New York, 1937. Reprinted by permission.

Racketeering exposed in connection with labor unions is in no sense peculiar to labor unions; it is part of a criminal pattern that has manifested itself in such diversified fields as prostitution, lottery and policy games, bail bonding, and in liquor traffic, both now and prior to repeal of the Eighteenth Amendment, as well as in legitimate forms of business activity. In each case the purpose is the unlawful extortion of tribute for the personal gain of a few individuals; in each case these individuals are found to be criminals who may be cloaked in the trappings of respectability but whose illegal activities are not confined to the labor racket.

One feature which is sometimes considered peculiar to labor racketeering is that the means employed may include practices not intrinsically illegal, namely, the threat of union sanctions such as strikes and picketing. But the threat of lawful action is made in connection with other types of extortion. . . .

That the means employed by the labor racketeer may not be unlawful makes it all the more important that the problem be approached with circumspection and with appreciation of the fact that labor racketeering is but a symptom of a far larger problem. Otherwise, proper efforts tending to bring into disrepute the lawful means employed by labor racketeers for unlawful ends may also tend to discredit legitimate labor activity for legitimate ends. . . .

"Labor racketeering" consists in essence of the use of a labor union by racketeers to exact payments to the racketeers from the employer, from members of the union, or from both. The racketeer may himself be a union official or he may operate from without the union either through his agents or through the exercise of coercion upon intimidated union officers. The labor racketeer is often enabled to maintain his dominant position through cooperation, passive or even active, on the part of the employer, whose inertia to the existence of a racket may be partially explained by the fact that the cost of the racket is usually passed on to the consumer, or to another branch of the industry, rather than borne by the employer himself. A further explanation may be found in the fact that the employer may actually profit by the racket. Thus, the employer may find it profitable to make periodic payments to a union officer in order to avoid compliance with a union rule, such as payment for overtime, or a requirement that members of the union shall not work with, or on the products of, nonunion labor. Or the employer may believe that the improvement of working conditions which may follow upon effective collective bargaining will cost him more than the labor racket.

III

BECK, HOFFA, AND THE TEAMSTERS UNION

Senator John L. McClellan of Arkansas headed a committee organized in 1956 to study criminal activities in the labor-management field. He later wrote a book describing the work of this Senate group which was instrumental in exposing such activities of leaders of the Teamsters Union. ☐ John L. McClellan, *Crime Without Punishment,* pp. 20–21, 39–41, 42. New York: Duell, Sloan and Pearce, copyright © 1962.

My criticism of labor leaders is directed only at those who drive for national power at the expense of the rest of our society; at those who are thieves and scoundrels; at those who cheat and lie to the dues paying rank-and-file members; at those who consort with gangsters; and at those who run their unions like feudal empires in total disregard of the traditionally fundamental democratic process. . . .

When he was elected to the presidency of the union in 1952, Beck pledged his honor to the task of safeguarding the funds of the membership and the integrity of the union. Yet during the five years of his term, he ignored the rights of the membership, carried out with greedy shamelessness a campaign to enrich himself from the treasury, and so neglected his duties that when he left office in disgrace, there were thugs and thieves in positions of power in the International Brotherhood.

We recall that his avariciousness became so widespread and so petty that he purchased five dozen diapers with union funds, presumably for a niece who had several children. . . .

Beck received kickbacks from placing Teamster mortgages with a company in which he had a financial interest. . . .

The testimony also showed that Beck received a twenty-four-thousand-dollar kickback when Shefferman [an associate of Beck's] supervised the interior decorating of the international headquarters, while also setting up a new bookkeeping system for the union. Shefferman's system was a singular one; with exasperating frequency during the long series of hearings on Teamster affairs, the committee's accountants found that records had been shifted for storage to cellars or attics, and then, according to testimony, thrown out as useless junk.

Beck pressured Anheuser-Busch, the St. Louis brewers, to favor a liquor distributing company whose president was none other than Dave Beck, Jr.

The committee heard testimony that a large part of the money that Beck repaid into the Teamster treasury was lent to him by the Fruehauf Trailer Company—a major supplier of the nation's commercial trailers, as should be evident to every motorist in the United States . . . .

Beck repaid the loan in full (with interest), in part from funds he realized when he sold his home in Seattle to the International Brotherhood of Teamsters for $163,215. The astonishing feature of this sale was that the house had been built in the first place with Teamster money. But that isn't all. After his retirement as president, Beck continued to live in the house. . . .

Beck and his son were tried and convicted of larceny, and Beck was convicted of filing fraudulent income-tax returns for a Teamster subsidiary.

The revulsion of the National Teamster membership caused Beck to step down as candidate for re-election to the presidency; he was burned in effigy by the members of a West Coast local.

Senator Robert F. Kennedy, the former Attorney General of the United States and the brother of the late President John F. Kennedy, served on the staff of the McClellan committee. After the conviction of Dave Beck, Kennedy's attention centered on James R. (Jimmy) Hoffa, who took Beck's place as head of the Teamsters Union. In 1964, Hoffa, too, was found guilty of malpractices by a federal court. □ *The Enemy Within* by Robert F. Kennedy, pp. 161–162. (New York: Harper and Brothers, 1960.) Copyright © 1960 by Robert F. Kennedy.

I am the first to admit that the record we uncovered is only a portion of the evil wrought by Hoffa, his men or associates. But what we did uncover shows clearly that the Teamster membership has been betrayed; democratic processes have been stifled; money, including pension and welfare funds, has been misused to the tune of at least $9,500,000; Hoffa and some of the men around him have got fat off enterprises they promoted with union backing. Perhaps worst of all, this potentially great institution, the Teamsters Union, has been turned over to the likes of Johnny Dio and Joey Glimco and Bert Brennan and Babe Triscaro and Sam Goldstein, and others who have spent their lives shifting in and out of the Teamsters and in and out of trouble with the law.

In 1957 Hoffa promised to clean up the Teamsters if he became president. In 1958 he said he had not had time to do a complete job. In 1959 he said the Teamsters were clean. Hoffa has abandoned any pretense that he will clean up. He has not—and because of the men around him, he cannot.

The Teamsters Union is the most powerful institution in this country—aside from the United States Government itself. In many major metropolitan areas the Teamsters control all transportation. It is a Teamster who drives the mother to the hospital at birth. It is the Teamster who drives the hearse at death. And between birth and burial, the Teamsters drive the trucks that clothe and feed us and provide the vital necessities of life. They control the pickup and deliveries of milk, frozen meat, fresh fruit, department store merchandise, newspapers, railroad express, air freight, and of cargo to and from the sea docks.

Quite literally your life—the life of every person in the United States—is in the hands of Hoffa and his Teamsters.

IV

UNION LEADERS SPEAK OUT

The Teamsters Union was expelled from the combined AFL-CIO at its convention in December 1957. In the following selection, George Meany, president of the AFL-CIO, explains the position of his organization toward labor racketeers and labor legislation. □ George Meany, *Power—For What?* pp. 11–12. Washington, D.C.: AFL-CIO Publication No. 97. Reprinted by permission.

The trade union movement met this problem head-on at the beginning of the AFL-CIO General Board in April, 1958. We pointed out we had taken effective and rigorous steps to clean house. We said we would go further and cooperate with Congress in the drafting of legislation to make it more difficult for anyone to misuse union funds.

Yes, we volunteered to cooperate in writing such legislation. But, we also said in April, 1958, that we will not accept punitive legislation designed to hurt the trade union movement under the guise of a law against corruption.

This was a truly significant action. Here was a group of private citizens saying to government: "We will assist you in writing legislation to regulate and govern certain of our actions." . . .

What other group in American life, business or professional, would, in the interests of morality, ethics and self-respect, cut off 10 percent of its membership and income as a self-enforcing action against those responsible for corruption?

The AFL-CIO did that very thing by expelling organizations whose leadership was found to be tainted.

Where is the business or banking association which has shown equal courage under similar circumstances? Show me any business organization which has set up a moral code for its membership which matches the Ethical Practices Codes adopted by the AFL-CIO.

Labor still stands on the position it took in April, 1958. We are still willing to cooperate—and we have cooperated—in drafting anti-corruption legislation, but we still make the reservation, and we will not withdraw from it, that we will not accept punitive or anti-labor legislation as part of this package.

Another prominent labor leader, James B. Carey, president of the International Union of Electrical, Radio and Machine Workers, also denounces racketeering and upholds the record of organized labor. □ James B. Carey, *Enemies Within the House of Labor.* Reprinted by permission of International Union of Electrical, Radio and Machine Workers.

We of the labor movement more than any other group changed the moral and ethical climate of our country. We made employers moral and made the government moral.

We made employers moral by compelling them to abandon their ancient dog-eat-dog economic philosophy and forcing them to accept the fact that labor is not a commodity but a grouping of individual human beings with the same rights, privileges and capacities as employers. We made employers moral by compelling them to understand that their responsibilities did not begin and end with profits but that they had inescapable social and economic obligations to the workers who created their wealth, their leisure and their luxuries.

We made the government moral by helping elect an administration responsive to the needs of the people and by erasing forever the concept of government as an instrument in the service of big business and industry. We made the government moral by insisting successfully, for the first time in history, that government has a responsibility to alleviate the mass unemployment, hunger and homelessness created by the free enterprise system. We made government moral by establishing its obligation to bring humanity and decency to the cut-throat economic jungle created by big business and industry. We made government moral by demonstrating that it had both the right and the duty to intervene in the prescription of minimum wages, maximum hours, healthful working conditions, the prohibition of child labor, the right to bargain collectively, old age security, and a host of other benefits and protections. . . .

Those who, either legally or illegally, use unionism solely as a means to personal enrichment deserve to be hounded out of the American labor movement as fast, as furiously and as finally as we can find the means to do it!

Such men are not unionists, but anti-unionists! They are not labor, but anti-labor! They are more dangerous to the democratic labor movement than the worst of union-hating managements! They are more poisonous than professional spies and strikebreakers! They are more destructive than the union-busting goon squads of two decades ago! They are more contaminating than any kind of decay that can afflict a labor union!

Because they betray us and our ideals from within the labor movement, they are doubly abominable and doubly dangerous. Because they exploit the sanctuary of union brotherhood to despoil the very name and idea of brotherhood, they bring a loathsome contagion into our midst.

We can fight reactionary employers and we can hold our own in combat with union-hating managements because we know pretty thoroughly where they stand. They don't pretend to be the opposite of what they are. They don't (at least not often these days) attempt to betray our organizations from within. Our fighting with management in recent years has become increasingly above-board. We know who our enemies are in the arena of economic conflict.

But we're not so sure today that we know who our enemies are within the labor movement. We know, however, that they are there, using the labor movement as a shield for their despicable practices. We know that trade unionism has been and is still being perverted into a protective cover for criminal activities.

The undeniable fact is that the House of Labor has termites and, therefore, needs a fumigation!

V

SENATOR JOHN F. KENNEDY ON RACKETEERS

John F. Kennedy, assassinated President of the United States, while a Massachusetts Senator sitting on the McClellan committee, offered the following recommendations as a result of the hearings. ☐ *U.S. Congress, Senate, 86th Congress, Report No. 1139,* Part 3, p. 510. "Final Report of the Select Committee on Improper Activities in the Labor or Management Field," March 28, 1960. Washington, D.C.: U.S. Government Printing Office, 1960.

In the modern criminal underworld we face a nationwide highly organized and highly effective internal enemy. The hearings demonstrated beyond a doubt that local law enforcement officers for various reasons were incapable of dealing with this enemy. In isolated areas of the country special police units have been set up to deal with racketeers. This they do admirably within their local jurisdiction. However, they are powerless to deal with interstate aspects of the problem. Worse than that, many local law enforcement agencies are either unable or unwilling to do any kind of a job of racketeer control.

Numerous expert witnesses have appeared before the committee and recommended that a National Crime Commission be established to deal with the underworld problem on a Federal level. Such a commission as proposed would gather information on the top criminal leaders of the country, keep a close surveillance on their activities, and disseminate their information to local and State law enforcement agencies. It would not have law enforcement powers, but merely act as a factor or intelligence gathering agency.

It seems to me that because of the nationwide aspects of this problem, a separate Federal agency should be established or an appropriate existing Federal agency be expanded or modified to act as an intelligence gathering agency on organized criminal activities.

Federal Regulation of Labor Unions

The outbreak of World War II united labor and management in defense of America. Soon after the declaration of war on December 8, 1941, leaders of industry and labor organizations gave President Roosevelt a voluntary pledge to forego lockouts and strikes during the emergency. A National War Labor Board was created in January 1942. This board provided a general wartime wage adjustment according to the so-called Little Steel formula which had given steelworkers an increase in wages based on a 15 per cent rise in the cost of living from January 1 to May 1, 1941.

Dissatisfied with this wage arrangement by 1943, the United Mine Workers' president, John L. Lewis, called a work stoppage on April 30th. President Roosevelt responded by ordering government seizure of coal mines. A crisis was averted when the miners were given wage increases in the form of allowances for travel time and compensation for shorter lunch periods. Later in the year, however, Congress passed the Smith-Connally Act authorizing the federal government to take over control of any plant where a work stoppage threatened the war effort.

Other restrictions on union activities were included in this legislation. In addition to this federal action, two states enacted right-to-work laws which prohibited union shop provisions in labor contracts. The provisions required all eligible employees to belong to unions. The trend which had begun in 1932 of broadening the powers of labor now seemed to be reversed.

With the coming of victory, a wave of postwar strikes prompted Republicans and conservative Democrats to declare that it was high time to "redress the balance of power" in the economy. Labor, it was claimed, had become too strong for the national good. Regulation of labor became a major issue in the Congressional election of 1946. The next year Congress passed the Taft-Hartley Act over the veto of President Harry S Truman. Designed to correct labor practices which, according to management, gave unions an unfair advantage, the new legislation curtailed the powers and activities of labor unions. The act, however, was labeled a "slave labor law" by organized workers.

Striving to fend off the new trend of legislation, labor unions plunged more deeply into political activities, following the traditional plan of the A.F. of L. "to defeat labor's enemies and to reward its friends." In 1955 the two major labor groups combined their strength and merged into a united organization called the AFL-CIO.

The readings which follow are concerned primarily with the controversy over the Taft-Hartley Act, officially known as the Labor Management Relations Act of 1947. As you read, think of these questions:

1   What was the source of power of John L. Lewis? Why did this power seem dangerous to the writer of the editorial in *The New York Times?*

2   What were the major provisions of the Taft-Hartley Act? Why did President Truman veto this measure? On what grounds did Senator Robert Taft defend it?

3   Why has the controversy over certain provisions of the Taft-Hartley Act lasted so long? What are the major parts of the law on which unions have concentrated their attacks? Why did they attack these parts?

I

CONDEMNING THE 1946 COAL STRIKE

The following editorial reflected the attitude of many Americans who felt that the strike weapon was being misused by organized labor. □ "Why We Have a Coal Strike," *The New York Times,* April 2, 1946, p. 26. Copyright © 1946, by The New York Times Company. Reprinted by permission.

Once more we are confronted by a nation-wide coal strike. In numbers of men involved it has been exceeded, since the end of the war, only by the strike in the steel industry. But it is potentially much more serious than that. A strike in the steel mills may tie up a hundred steel-using industries; but a strike in the coal mines can tie up the steel mills. And it affects railroads and public utilities far more quickly than a steel strike. Once more the country will learn the meaninglessness of measuring strikes by the number of men directly involved. They can be measured only by their whole effect on our organically interdependent economy. From this standpoint no walkout can strike a blow closer to the heart of an industrial economy than one in the coal mines.

John L. Lewis knows all this. It is the very source of his power. . . .

. . . Rather than denounce Mr. Lewis, it will be more profitable to examine the source of his power. It is in large part the product of Federal labor policy. The United Mine Workers were extremely weak in 1933. They were built up first by the NRA labor sections, then by the Wagner Act and the Guffey Coal Act. Under the Wagner Act the employers are compelled to conduct collective bargaining in good faith, but the union leaders are under no such compulsion—which helps to explain the vagueness of Mr. Lewis' demands and his contemptuous attitude toward the employers' representatives in the last few weeks. . . .

. . . He knows that not in years has the Federal Government stood up on principle against any strike demand backed by a sufficiently powerful union. He knows that the unions in recent years have almost invariably got more from the Federal Government by striking than by not striking.

II

TRUMAN ON THE TAFT-HARTLEY ACT

In June 1947 Congress passed the Taft-Hartley Act. President Truman's prompt veto expressed his strong conviction that the nation had more to lose than to gain by this legislation. In the following selection he summarizes his views. □ Harry S Truman, *Memoirs,* Vol. 2, pp. 29–30. Garden City, N.Y.: Doubleday and Co., Inc. Copyright © 1956 by Time, Incorporated.

On labor legislation, also, there was a wide gap between the Congress and the President. . . . [Anti-labor] sentiment, inflamed by John L. Lewis' defiance of the government in the fall of 1946, was gaining new strength, and labor legislation became a prime issue in 1947.

On January 6, 1947, in the State of the Union message, I had urged legislation to deal with the basic causes of labor-management difficulties. Specifically warning against punitive legislation under the stress of emotions created by the recent strife in which not only labor and management but the government and the public had been embroiled, I proposed a four-point program:

1. The early enactment of legislation to prevent certain unjustifiable practices, such as jurisdictional strikes, secondary boycotts, and the use of economic forces by either labor or management to decide issues arising out of existing contracts.

2. The extension of the facilities within the Department of Labor for assisting collective bargaining—integration of governmental machinery to provide the successive steps of mediation, voluntary arbitration, and ascertainment of the facts.

3. A broadening of the program of social legislation to alleviate the causes of workers' . . . [insecurity]—extension of social security, better housing, a national health program, and provision for a fair minimum wage.

4. The appointment of a Temporary Joint Commission to inquire into the field of labor-management relations.

This program offered a sound approach to the nation's industrial problems. But the Eightieth Congress began to hammer out the wrong kind of legislation.

Representative Fred Hartley, Jr., of New Jersey, chairman of the House Labor Committee, introduced a bill which was passed by the House in April. This drastic strike-curb bill, while it contained some good points, was an extremist measure which would abolish the National Labor Relations Board and substitute a Labor-Management Relations Board, make illegal industry-wide strikes, the closed shop, jurisdictional and sympathy strikes, mass picketing, all strikes by government workers, deprive violating unions of their bargaining rights for one year, deprive unlawful strikers of their right to get their jobs back, make unions suable, require unions to make financial reports, and empower the President to obtain injunctions against strikes in interstate transportation, communications, or public utilities.

A similar bill was being formulated in the Senate by the Labor Committee headed by Senator Robert Taft of Ohio. In May a ten-man Senate-House conference committee began combining the Taft bill with the Hartley bill.

The amended Labor-Management Relations Act of 1947, better known as the Taft-Hartley Act, was sent to the White House for my signature on June 18. Two days later I vetoed the act. The veto message listed the objections to it: The bill was completely contrary to our national policy of economic freedom because it would result in more or less government intervention into the collective-bargaining process. Because of its legal complexities the act would become a source of time-consuming litigation which would encourage distrust and bitterness between labor and management. The bill was neither workable nor fair. The Taft-Hartley bill would go far toward weakening our trade-union movement by injecting political considerations into normal economic decisions. . . .

The Senate overruled my veto on June 23, and the Labor-Management Relations Act of 1947 became the law of the land. I had done all within my power to prevent an injustice against the laboring men and women of the United States.

In more specific terms, President Truman voiced his reasons for disapproving the Taft-Hartley Act. The following is from a newspaper summary of his veto message. □ "High Points of Message," *The New York Times,* June 21, 1947, p. 2. New York: The Associated Press, copyright © 1947.

1. The bill would allow the Government to get court orders to block national strikes affecting public health or safety during eighty days of mediation.

TRUMAN: "This procedure would be certain to do more harm than good, and to increase rather than diminish widespread industrial disturbances."

2. The bill would forbid the closed shop, in which the employer can hire only union help.

TRUMAN: "The bill disregards the voluntary development in the field of industrial relations in the United States over the past 150 years. Today over 11,000,000 workers are employed under some type of union-security contract. The great majority of the plants which have such union security provisions have had few strikes."

3. The bill would ban certain kinds of boycotts.

TRUMAN: "It would deprive workers of the power to meet the competition of goods produced under sweatshop conditions by permitting employers to halt every type of secondary boycott, not merely those for justifiable purposes."

4. The bill would ban certain kinds of strikes.

TRUMAN: "The bill would make it an unfair labor practice to 'induce or encourage' certain types of strikes and boycotts—and then would forbid the National Labor Relations Board to consider as evidence 'views, argument or opinion' by which such a charge could be proved."

5. The bill would permit court suits against unions that break contracts.

TRUMAN: "It would give employers the means to engage in endless litigation, draining the energy and resources of unions in court actions, even though the particular charges were groundless."

6. The bill would deny collective-bargaining rights to any union having as an officer a Communist or anyone who could "reasonably be regarded" as one.

TRUMAN: "Congress intended to assist labor organizations to rid themselves of Communist officers; with this objective I am in full accord. (But) I am convinced that the bill would have an effect exactly opposite to that intended by the Congress."

III

SENATOR TAFT ANSWERS PRESIDENT TRUMAN

Responding to President Truman's criticism of the Taft-Hartley Act, Senator Robert A. Taft of Ohio stoutly defended its provisions. □ Radio address by Senator Taft. *The New York Times*, June 21, 1947, p. 4. Copyright © 1947, by The New York Times Company. Reprinted by permission.

The President's message vetoing the Labor Bill was a complete misrepresentation of both the general character of the bill and of most of its detailed provisions. . . .

Remember that this bill was considered in detail by both Houses of Congress for five months. Every provision was worked over and debated first in the committee, several times on the floor of the Senate, and then in Congress. . . .

. . . The President ignored the opinion and studied conclusion of the Democrats in the House of Representatives, who voted 106 to 71 this afternoon to override his veto.

On the contrary, the President has apparently adopted in large part the prejudiced arguments of the union labor leaders who from the beginning have opposed any legislation whatever and refused to cooperate with Congress or make any constructive suggestions.

The President's message follows in many details the analysis of the bill prepared by . . . [the] general counsel of the CIO . . . .

President Truman wholly ignored the detailed arguments . . . which I presented on the floor of the United States Senate. Following the lead of union labor leaders, the President does not find a single good provision in the entire bill.

If there is one subject on which every unprejudiced person is agreed, it is that unions must be made responsible for their acts: that collective bargaining cannot continue to be an important factor in our labor relations unless both parties are bound by their contracts.

The President criticizes every provision designed to make unions responsible. He criticizes the requirement that they file financial and other reports with the Department of Labor.

Corporations have long been required to file reports both with State and local authorities. Why not unions?

He attacks the provisions that unions may be sued for breach of collective bargaining agreements, on the ground that they should not be bothered with having to defend lawsuits regardless of what they do.

He says they might be harassed by suits by an employer. Everybody else in the United States is subject to harassment by lawsuits. Why not unions? In any event, the purpose of this provision is to induce them to live up to their contracts, and if they do, few suits if any will ever be filed.

The President attacks the section permitting an injunction against the nation-wide strike affecting the national health and safety. It was through such a procedure he secured an injunction against John L. Lewis last fall. Last year when faced by a nation-wide strike, it was the President himself who recommended Government seizure and the drafting of all the strikers into the United States Army.

Because Congress now gives him a carefully considered authority to allay such a strike, to attempt mediation, and finally to conduct a strike vote when other remedies have been exhausted, he says the procedure will do more harm than good.

He prefers to let the Smith-Connally Act expire on June 30 without any protection whatever to the people against nation-wide strikes. He claims that this bill would breed too much intervention in our economic life, and imposes Government control over free, collective bargaining.

The bill in no way interferes with the rights of the parties to bargain, in no way limits the right to strike if they fail to agree, except in the case of a nation-wide strike for a period of eighty days until an election can be held.

Organized labor reacted swiftly and bitterly to passage of the Taft-Hartley Act over President Truman's veto. ☐ Charles Grutzner, "Miners Walk Out," *The New York Times,* June 24, 1947, p. 1. Copyright © 1947, by The New York Times Company. Reprinted by permission.

More than 18,000 of the nation's 400,000 soft coal miners stopped work yesterday within a few hours after the Taft-Hartley labor measure became law over the President's veto.

About 8,600 men quit the pits in Pennsylvania, more than 6,000 in Alabama, 2,600 in West Virginia and 1,500 in Ohio, according to The Associated Press.

Leaders of the American Federation of Labor, the Congress of Industrial Organizations and independent unions all over the country announced their intention to test the new law on picket lines and in the courts. A prediction that 90 per cent of all organized labor would go on a protest strike within a week was made in Birmingham, Ala., by R. E. Farr, district president of the United Steelworkers of America, CIO.

A nation-wide work stoppage for twenty-four hours in protest against what was termed the "slave law" was urged by the San Francisco CIO Council in a telegram to Philip Murray, president of the CIO. Earlier, Mr. Murray had called a meeting for Friday in Washington of the CIO executive board. Lee Pressman, general counsel, summoned legal representatives of every CIO union to the nation's capital.

William Green, president of the AFL, announced the start of a campaign to induce members of Congress to repeal the act, which he warned would produce "chaotic conditions," reduce industrial production and "endanger our national economy."

An editorial in *The New York Times* surveyed the question of implementing the Taft-Hartley Act through a hostile administration and suggested that labor may not find it so bad, after all. ☐ "The Labor Bill Becomes Law," *The New York Times,* June 24, 1947, p. 22. Copyright © 1947, by The New York Times Company. Reprinted by permission.

As an ironical result of the system of separation of powers in our Government and of the Executive's independence of the Legislature, the task of administering the new law will now go to an Administration which does not believe in it and to a President who has just denounced it as unworkable. This is hardly an auspicious start. Yet we may well hope and believe that Mr. Truman and his executive assistants will give the new law a fair and a full trial, in all good faith. . . .

We may also hope that union labor, while not yielding in any way its unquestioned right to seek the repeal of this legislation through the election of new members of Congress favorable to such action, will nevertheless pay it the same respect that union labor quite properly asked of employers in the case of the Wagner Act when that measure took its place on the statute books a dozen years ago. Now that the immediate political necessity has passed of describing this law in such hysterical terms as "slave labor legislation," it may well be that union labor will find in it much that is useful and advantageous—for example, its reaffirmation of all the essential rights of collective bargaining and its relisting of "unfair labor practices" on the part of employers, outlawed under the Wagner Act and again outlawed now.

IV

THE FIGHT GOES ON

Ten years after passage of the Taft-Hartley Act, organized labor continued to object to its provisions. The following selection, from a pamphlet published by the AFL-CIO, reflects this attitude. □ *Industrial Unions and Taft-Hartley*, pp. 8–9. Washington, D.C.: Industrial Union Department. Pamphlet No. 9, June 1957.

Taft-Hartley attacks the very heart of the American trade union movement by restricting collective bargaining and legitimate organizing activities.

In the area of collective bargaining, the Act turned back the clock to the day of the hated and discredited theory of government by injunction. The so-called "national emergency injunction" has had, in the words of the Federal Mediation and Conciliation Service, "the effect of interfering with collective bargaining" and "tends to delay rather than facilitate settlement."

The right of workers to picket has been seriously challenged. The right to strike has been abridged and the right to vote in Labor Board elections has been denied strikers and turned over to strikebreakers. Perhaps even more important, Taft-Hartley has enabled reactionary employers to oppose the organization of their employees with campaigns of subtle and open intimidation.

If this were not enough, Taft-Hartley also makes possible endless and unnecessary delays in the functioning of the National Labor Relations Board. Following the old axiom that justice delayed is justice denied, some employers have made use of these anti-union devices to stall, harass, and ultimately defeat union organization.

Strewn throughout the Act are these provisions and others aimed at restricting unionism. That Taft-Hartley has not destroyed the labor movement is true, but for its existence the labor movement owes no thanks to the law. That our nation's unions have survived under Taft-Hartley is a testimonial to their strength and to the determination of American workers to maintain their union organizations.

V

ATTACK ON RIGHT-TO-WORK LAWS

No single feature of the Taft-Hartley Act aroused so much vehement and persistent opposition from labor organizations as its provisions allowing states to pass their own right-to-work laws. These enactments, forbidding inclusion of union-shop clauses in labor contracts, were considered a threat to the very foundation of unionism. The final selection measures the success of these right-to-work laws. □ *Facts vs. Propaganda—The Truth About "Right-to-Work" Laws,* AFL-CIO Publication No. 46, December 1958. Reprinted by permission.

But "right-to-work" laws throw a roadblock in the path of union organization.

Most of the states where industry and commerce have grown fastest, and prospered most, have no "right-to-work" law. There is no "right-to-work" law, for instance, in such big industrial states as New York, California, Michigan, Ohio, Illinois, Pennsylvania or Massachusetts—to name only a few.

In Massachusetts, for example, members of both parties of the state legislature joined to defeat a "right-to-work" law proposal by a vote of 190 to 2.

Most of the states that have "right-to-work" laws have comparatively little industry. Supporters of this kind of legislation argue that passage of "right-to-work" laws will attract industry and raise wages. But their arguments just don't hold up against the facts, as revealed in the official statistics.

In Mississippi, factory workers earned an average of only $50.00 a week in 1955. Per capita personal income—the average personal income of every man, woman and child—in that "right-to-work" state was only $946.00 a year, the lowest in the nation.

In "right-to-work" South Carolina, the average weekly earnings of factory workers were $53.00 in 1955. They were $54.00 in Georgia, another "right-to-work" state. Per capita personal income in South Carolina was $1,108 for the year, and in Georgia it was $1,333.

Here are some cases where a "right-to-work" law didn't produce the utopian economic results that its sponsors claimed would benefit the average people. All the law did was destroy union security.

These per capita income figures are far below the national average. What the figures show is that no state "can get rich quick" by adopting a "right-to-work" law.

The road to greater wealth is through the development of industry, with cooperative labor-management relations, including the opportunity to agree on union security.

When there is good faith and trust—as exemplified by union security agreements—the obstacles are cleared away from the road to understanding, higher production and improved economic conditions for workers, employers—and, indeed, to all the community.

PROBLEM 15

Automation and Collective Bargaining

Since 1945 two critical developments have become the focus of attention in discussions about the future of American labor. The first of these is the problem of adapting the labor force to technological innovations known as "automation." The second question concerns the place of collective bargaining in a modern economy.

Mechanization of industry has been going on as long as there has been a labor movement. Automation, however, has added new dimensions to the process by providing automatic controls to transfer materials from one process to another and by furnishing electronic devices for decision-making. Thus, the machine is not only replacing man's muscle, but in many areas the machine performs as well those mental jobs which do not require inventiveness and ingenuity.

Some unions responded to this threat of rapidly diminishing needs for labor by insisting on retaining old contractual rules that were made before modern equipment and methods were introduced. Management has resisted this arrangement, attacking such rules as "featherbedding" in which employers are compelled to pay wages for little or no work. On the other hand, many unions have bowed to the inevitable, accepting mechanization and seeking to compensate for loss of jobs with a greater share of economic benefits for their remaining workers.

The growth of automation has also brought into question the relevance in a modern economy of traditional methods of collective bargaining. Some persons say that the delicately balanced modern industrial system no longer lends itself to settlement of disputes through the give and take of bargaining methods. What is needed, it is said, is a system of compulsory arbitration with government acting as judge to settle differences. Would this remedy be worse than the disease? The answer to this, as well as to many other questions posed by these Problems, lies in the future.

The selections which follow concern automation, featherbedding, and the future of collective bargaining. As you read, consider these questions:

1 What problem does automation bring to American workers? Does automation create as many jobs as it abolishes? Can the same people who are replaced by new machines take the new jobs which these machines create? What problem does this situation pose for the economy?

2 What is the attitude of John L. Lewis toward automation? Does this attitude seem fair to all concerned?

3 In what way does featherbedding seem an answer to automation? Is it an economical answer? Why might railroad workers support such methods? What should be done about this problem?

4 Why did railroad brotherhoods oppose arbitration of their dispute with the railroad owners over featherbedding? Why did they prefer to depend on traditional collective bargaining procedures? Why did Walter Lippmann declare that the country had outgrown traditional collective bargaining methods?

I

AUTOMATION AND UNEMPLOYMENT

Problems of unemployment prompted the following newspaper account dealing with the historical impact of automation. □ Jack W. Germond, "The Unemployment Problem," *Rochester Times-Union*, March 12, 1963, p. 7. Rochester, N.Y.: The Gannett Newspapers, copyright © 1963.

The nation's stubborn unemployment problem is threatening to get a great deal worse before it gets any better.

While the economy is limping forward, creating new jobs in dribs and drabs, two counter trends that will add to the labor surplus are careening along with increasing momentum. One is the mechanization of industry that is wiping out jobs on all sides.

The other is the swelling of the labor force as the post-war baby crop moves out of the classrooms and into the job market.

Unless there is a dramatic quickening of the economy's pace, these trends may become so dominant that unemployment levels that were the high points of recessions just a few years ago will become what will be considered normal in the years ahead.

Young people are entering the labor force at a rate 40 per cent faster during the 1960's than they did during the 1950's. In 1970, some 3.8 million youngsters will reach 18, compared to 2.6 million in 1960.

The result: The economy must produce 13½ million new jobs in this decade just to keep pace with the growth in the labor force, without cutting into the backlog of 4 million already out of work.

To this can be added whatever job losses result from mechanization and gains in productivity. According to one labor department analysis, this might amount to another 200,000 a year.

In short, the economy will be challenged to produce 25,000 to 30,000 new jobs a week when it has not even been able to add 15,000.

In the last 5 years the net gains and losses in the private sector of the economy have just about canceled one another out. New full-time jobs in trade, finance, insurance, real estate and service industries have been largely offset by losses in agriculture, mining, construction, manufacturing, transportation and utilities. . . .

The elimination of jobs in the private sector can be charged to several factors.

One is changes in consumer patterns, such as the swing from railroad to air travel. Another is the problem of foreign competition.

But the key has been the growing efficiency of industry and the production of more goods with less labor through automation.

(Automation has two definitions: In the strict sense, the term applies only to advanced, self-correcting mechanized systems. But in the sense now more generally accepted, it applies to any major technological improvement.)

Just how much automation will mean in the years ahead is impossible to forecast with any accuracy. Computers can guide rockets into space, collect eggs and operate machine tools, but they can't predict their own future impact.

Some indication can be gained, however, from the record of the past. Industrial productivity—in output per man hour of labor—has risen 50 per cent since 1947.

A ton of steel is being produced with only two-thirds the labor required in 1951. Bakeries are wrapping 7,000 loaves of bread an hour with two men, compared to 4,000 loaves with seven men just a few years ago. Payroll computers are doing the work of 28 office workers. . . .

A top executive of one of the world's largest corporations put it this way:

"Of course we're responsible for jobs being eliminated. Every time we put in a new machine, it suggests other steps we can take. There's no question but that it will speed up. . . ."

Perhaps more important than opinions or case histories, however, is the overwhelming logic that argues for faster mechanization.

Automation offers dramatic savings to some firms. A chemical company reports savings of $50,000 to $150,000 a year from instruments costing $10,000 to $15,000. A plastics firm saves $33,000 a year from automatic controls costing $24,500. And a power company saves $400,000 a year by using a $100,000 computer to plan the distribution of its load.

American industries are under continuing pressure to take such steps if they are to compete with others at home and abroad. In foreign trade particularly, there is a compelling need to reduce unit costs.

And finally, in many industries management feels pressures—real or imagined—to lessen its dependence on its workers and union leadership. . . .

The central argument made for automation is that it creates as many jobs as it abolishes. The theory is that, in the long run, mechanization will mean largely a shift from blue-collar to white-collar jobs.

This trend already is quite pronounced, but there are two flaws in the theory.

First, the number of workers added in the offices is not likely to match the number dropped in the plants. In the last 5 years, manufacturing industries have added 335,000 nonproduction workers to the payrolls while cutting their production forces by 969,000.

Second, the same workers are not involved in most cases. Few production workers are qualified for white collar work and many are considered too lacking in education or too old to train.

Perhaps the most authoritative word on the automation-jobs relationship has come from Thomas J. Watson, president of International Business Machines Corp., the giant of the computer industry.

In a statement to a congressional committee during the last recession, Watson said:

"We can't argue that technological change and automation are not labor-saving processes. Of course they are. They do cause displacement of people. In fact, to do so is one of their major purposes. They may also upgrade people or increase the prosperity of an industry so that more are employed. Nevertheless, we do have more unemployment than we can tolerate today and some of it has come from technological change and automation."

II

HOW THE MINE WORKERS FACED MECHANIZATION

For more than five decades the United Mine Workers have followed a general policy of adjustment to increased mechanization of coal mining. John L. Lewis, president of the organization during the greater part of this period, very early accepted the inevitability of a reduced work force. In the selection which follows he discusses some compensations for these losses. ☐ John L. Lewis. Quoted in the *United Mine Workers Journal.* Washington, D.C.: October 1952, pp. 20, 44.

The theory of the trade unions is that the manufacturer must either equip his factory with modern labor-saving devices or else suffer by competition, but that he may not pay lower wages because of his unwillingness to secure the best machinery. Where trade unions do not exist, employers with the worst and oldest machinery and the most antiquated methods manage to eke out a precarious existence by underpaying and starving their workmen, but where trade unionism is able to enforce a definite minimum wage, these less skillful and less adequately equipped manufacturers must either introduce modern appliances or go to the wall. As a consequence, the countries, the industries, and even the individual establishments where trade unionism is strongest are those in which machinery is applied earliest and to the largest extent. . . .

At the outset, we must recognize the undisputed fact that mechanization has done its work; that there is no hope for the re-employment of millions of our unemployed under the present day industrial relationship; that robots do not consume goods; that American workmen, by their efficient utilization of machines, have so multiplied their productivity that they have earned the right to enjoy the six-hour day and five-day week; furthermore, that the rates of minimum wages paid for such employment shall constitute a family standard commensurate with an American mode of living.

Organized labor further insists that if industry is to persist in discarding men at the age of forty-five, our accepted scheme of industrial relations must be based upon such a tenure of employment, or society accept in lieu thereof the responsibility of caring for those thus thrown into the scrap heap of human want and despair.

Lewis' claims for leadership in fostering mechanization are stated in the following excerpt. □ *United Mine Workers Journal,* October 1952, pp. 237, 239–240.

The American coal operators never would have mechanized their mines unless they had been compelled to do so by the organization of the mine workers. The UMWA holds that labor is entitled to a participation in the increased productivity due to mechanization. We decided the question of displacement of workers by mechanization years ago. We decided it is better to have a half a million men working in the industry at good wages and high standards of living, than it is to have a million working in the industry in poverty and degradation.

There can be no increase in the standard of living in America except as we create new values by increased productivity. . . .

You know, in our form of economy, there are three parties to benefit as a result of these improved techniques—a new chemical formula, a new invention, a new process. I am among those who do not believe that God ever put an idea in the mind of an inventor for the sole advantage of an employer. The parties to benefit from that improved technique and that increased productivity are: the investor and the employer who has his investment made more secure and more profitable; the worker who is able to have a higher wage, shorter hours, improved conditions and greater protection against evil days; and, the public which draws its reward from having a unit of manufacture at lesser cost.

The United Mine Workers of America desire that the distribution of the advantages and benefits of the machine shall not be restricted to the few, but that all of the personnel in the coal industry shall participate and be on a more or less equal level. The narrow wage differential between skilled and more highly skilled miners comes about as a matter of deliberate policy.

A man gets $19 a day now for running a modern continuous cutting machine. We see no reason why he should be raised to $23 a day merely because the machine has raised productivity, because that would mean that we would have $4 less to distribute elsewhere around the mine. You can't keep some men in the classification of pot boys or janitors, while you make another man in the same mine a preferred citizen by allowing him a higher rate. As a matter of fact, and in the realm of human relations, you merely make him an agent of the company, who will conspire with management to get wage increases for himself, to the great detriment of the mass of men employed.

III

RAILROADS AND TECHNOLOGICAL UNEMPLOYMENT

The response of the railroad unions to mechanization has been quite different from that of Lewis' coal miners. In 1963 suspension of traditional work rules on railroad lines threatened a nation-wide strike. The following selection indicates the position of the interested parties. ☐ John D. Pomfret, "Showdown on the Railroads," *The New York Times*, July 7, 1963, p. 4E. Copyright © 1963, by The New York Times Company. Reprinted by permission.

Mr. Loomis [president of the Association of American Railroads] charged that "featherbedding"—which he defined as "pay for work not done, for services not performed"—was a "festering and cancerous growth" that was ruining the railroads to the tune of $500,000,000 a year.

Mr. Loomis announced that the railroads planned to fight the unions to obtain changes in work rules to allow elimination of allegedly unneeded employes. . . .

H. E. Gilbert, president of the Brotherhood of Locomotive Firemen and Enginemen, shrugged off Mr. Loomis's remarks. "Featherbedding," he said, "is the straw man that the railroads create each time wage negotiations are due. . . ."

The rules changes proposed by the railroads would eliminate 37,000 firemen in freight and yard service and as many as 19,000 trainmen and yard helpers by giving the railroads a free hand in determining manning needs. The rules also would give the carriers freedom to rearrange runs to get more work from some employes, thus cutting manpower needs further. Finally, the carriers want to revise the pay structure . . . .

Although the five unions representing engineers, firemen, trainmen, conductors and switchmen have made demands of their own, theirs has been essentially a fight to maintain the status quo. In contrast to the usual bargaining controversy, management here has held the initiative all the way.

The heart of the matter is that the issues involve eliminating thousands of jobs at a time when they are fast disappearing anyway.

Total employment in the industry—2,000,000 in 1920—declined from 1,400,000 in 1947 to 800,000 in 1960 and now stands at about 700,000. The number of operating employes declined from 807,000 to 212,000 between 1947 and 1960—a 31 per cent drop and now stands at below 200,000.

Dwindling business, much of it lost to trucks and airlines, caused some of the employment decline. But much was due to technological change of staggering impact.

The principal one has been the switch from steam to the diesel locomotive. This has reduced repairs and made possible longer trains and longer runs, cutting sharply the number of operating employes needed.

Had severe technological change been accompanied by booming business, it is possible that the railroads and the operating unions would have worked out their differences. But lagging revenues and changing technology have coincided. This has meant that the railroads have been determined to get the full benefit of labor-saving devices, and the workers, confronted by insecurity and unemployment outside the industry as well as inside, have been equally determined to hang on to their jobs.

There is a third interest that has complicated the bargaining—that of the unions as institutions. Declining membership means declining dues, income, influence and power. It puts in jeopardy the jobs of officials and staff.

IV

COLLECTIVE BARGAINING OR GOVERNMENT ARBITRATION?

The following news article goes to the core of the question concerning the future of collective bargaining in an automated society. □ Donald Janson, "Rail Firemen See Jobs Doomed," *The New York Times,* August 11, 1963, p. 1. Copyright © 1963, by The New York Times Company. Reprinted by permission.

Four years ago the carriers announced their intention to eliminate "featherbedding" or unneeded jobs. The largest group to go would be 40,000 firemen . . . .

Although individual firemen are reluctant to say so for attribution, they expect that the long-range solution to be no dismissals but an end to employment of replacements. . . .

But even with a crisis at hand, they are not willing to concede officially that all firemen's jobs in freight and yard service must go. And they are completely unwilling to have the impasse arbitrated by neutrals.

They are equally unwilling to have a settlement imposed by Congress, but they seem to be resigned to accepting one if it comes.

They say that opposition to arbitration is not a matter of lack of confidence in the merits of their position but a matter of fundamental principle.

If unions surrendered their right to negotiate contracts, they say, it would be the beginning of the end for collective bargaining and the right to strike.

"The only reason a union exists is to negotiate through collective bargaining a working agreement on wages and conditions of employment," a spokesman asserted, continuing:

"Any impasse that results must be settled by economic force. On our side, this means strikes. For almost a century, this is what the whole American labor movement has been built on.

"Professors or men of judicial standing or other neutrals cannot substitute for the people involved in writing an agreement. Unions would be surrendering their responsibility to permit it.

"There is no such thing as a temporary surrender that would affect just this case or any other single case. Once unions allowed arbitration it would become a matter of practice."

The famous political analyst Walter Lippmann succinctly summarizes the position of labor, management, and the government in the changing industrial picture. ☐ Walter Lippmann, "Compulsory Arbitration," Washington, D.C.: *The Washington Post*, August 20, 1963, p. A13.

The railroad dispute has been going on for four years because in an essential industry the existing machinery of labor relations can no longer be made to work.

The theory of free collective bargaining has been that the railroads and the unions would bargain until they agreed, the unions deriving their bargaining power from their willingness to strike and the railroads from their ability to outlast the unions when the trains stopped running. . . .

The theory of free collective bargaining in key industries has broken down because neither party to a dispute can any longer use its bargaining power. The sanctions behind the bargaining power—the strike and the lockout—can no longer be tolerated by the national government. They are in fact outlawed.

· A national stoppage is intolerable, and in one way or another a nationwide strike or a lockout will be broken. Thus, the innerspring of free collective bargaining is, as regards key industries, dismantled.

The country has outgrown the existing machinery for dealing with big labor disputes. But the country has not yet grown up to a consensus on the machinery to replace it. When a new system of industrial relations is established, it is bound to consist of some form of judicial inquiry and judgment. . . .

We may say then that the old system of labor relations with strikes and lockouts is obsolete for the key industries, and that eventually it is going to be replaced by a system of compulsory arbitration.

Glossary of Labor Terms

ARBITRATION   Referral of a labor dispute to a third party or agency for settlement.

AUTOMATION   Process of making machines self-regulating, and also the use of such automatic devices.

BLACKLIST   List of names of union members, circulated among employers, to prevent those on the list from obtaining jobs.

BOYCOTT   Refusal of workers to buy goods or services from a hostile employer. *See* Secondary boycott.

CHECK-OFF   Privilege of unions to have management automatically deduct union dues from workers' wages without written consent of workers. Illegal under Taft-Hartley Act.

CLOSED SHOP   Establishment where only union workers are employed. Outlawed under Taft-Hartley Act.

COLLECTIVE BARGAINING   Organized effort of workers through representatives of their own choice for dealing with employers to determine wages, hours, and working conditions.

COMPANY UNION   Labor organization which is created and controlled by management.